BRADSHAW'S GUIDE TO SCOTLAND'S RAILWAYS PART 2:

BERWICK TO ABERDEEN & BEYOND

Campbell McCutcheon

AMBERLEY

Fond Delusion
First Tourist (going North). 'Hullo, Tompk...'

Second Tourist (ditto). 'Hsh—sh! Confound it, you'll spoil all. They think in the train I'm a Highland chief!'

About this book

Bradshaw's Guide explores many aspects of the railway journeys to be had on Scotland's railways. Through Bradshaw's text and the supportive images, the lines are described, and main features shown. Of course, some of the lines have been closed and others have opened since Bradshaw compiled this guide in 1863. Hopefully, it will encourage you to delve into the history of the railways of Scotland and encourage you to visit some otherwise bypassed town. Please note that public access to railway lines is restricted for reasons of safety.

First published 2014

Amberley Publishing
The Hill, Stroud
Gloucestershire, GL5 4EP

www.amberley-books.com

Copyright © Campbell McCutcheon and John Christopher, 2014

The right of Campbell McCutcheon and John Christopher to be identified as the Author of this work has been asserted in accordance with the Copyrights, Designs and Patents Act 1988.

ISBN 978 1 4456 3623 8
ISBN 978 1 4456 3651 1 (ebook)

British Library Cataloguing in Publication Data.
A catalogue record for this book is available from the British Library.

Typeset in 9.5pt on 12pt Celeste.
Typesetting by Amberley Publishing.
Printed in the UK.

Bradshaw on Scotland

A haggis is a pudding exclusively Scotch, but considered of French origin. Its ingredients are oatmeal, suet, pepper, &c., and it is usually boiled in a sheep's stomach. Although a heavy, yet it is by no means a disagreeable dish.

Bradshaw's vivid and obviously agreeable description of the haggis is just one of the interesting anecdotes and descriptions that lift *Bradshaw's Descriptive Railway Hand-Book of Great Britain and Ireland* from a tome describing the railway routes in existence north of the border in 1863 to a genuine informative guidebook of the most important places in Scotland. This book is one of a series published by Amberley which helps bring Bradshaw into the twenty-first century, giving the reader a font that is readable and a breadth of illustrative material that help to portray the Scotland that the Bradshaw's Guide writers would have seen on their travels in 1861–63 as they compiled the guide. Two parts bring the Scotland of the 1860s to life, with this, the second, primarily concerning itself with the east coast and Borders, and part one covering what we now know as the West Coast Main Line and the railways of western Scotland. Ultimately, the series, which already covers the lines of Isambard Kingdom Brunel, the Great Western Railway and the South East of England, will encompass all of the railways of the United Kingdom and of Ireland.

Below: Railway chart for the Edinburgh, Granton, Haymarket and Leith area, 1905.

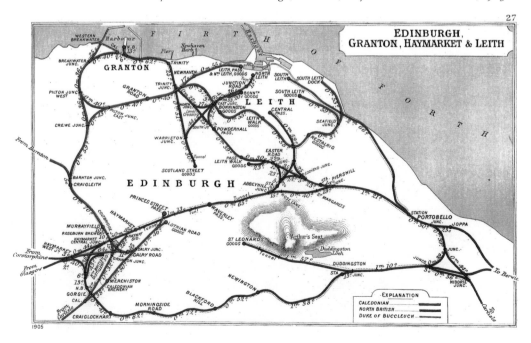

Bradshaw and Scotland

George Bradshaw was born in 1801 and died in 1853 at the age of fifty-two. His publishing empire had begun in the canal age, and he produced a series of maps and guides of Britain's canals. With the advent of the railways, his attention turned to guides to the new form of transport and, by 1863, his guide covered the whole of the United Kingdom. Scotland itself had some of Britain's oldest railways, from the KIlmarnock & Troon to the Garnkirk & Glasgow. The Kilmarnock & Troon was one of the pioneer railways to operate a locomotive hauled service, predating both the Stockton & Darlington and the Liverpool & Manchester Railways. By the 1860s, mineral rich Scotland was criss-crossed by railway routes, with lines branching into the Highlands, as well as to the main ferry ports on the west coast. Still to come were such engineering marvels as the Tay and Forth railway bridges, although the Royal Border Bridge at Berwick-upon-Tweed had already opened, completing the route from Newcastle to Edinburgh.

It is fair to say that the railways are the Victorians' greatest legacy to the twentieth and twenty-first centuries. They shrank space and time. Before their coming different parts of the country had existed in local time based on the position of the sun, with Bristol, for example, running ten minutes behind London. The Great Western Railway changed all that in 1840 when it applied synchronised railway time throughout its area. The presence of the railways defined the shape and development of many of our towns and cities, they altered the distribution of the population and forever changed the fundamental patterns of our lives. For many millions of Britons the daily business of where they live and work, and travel between the two, is defined by the network of iron rails laid down nearly two centuries ago by the engineers and an anonymous army of railway navvies.

The timing of the publication of Bradshaw's guidebooks is interesting. This particular account is taken from the 1863 edition of the handbook although, for practical reasons, it must have been written slightly earlier, probably between 1860 and 1862. By this stage the railways had lost their pioneering status, and with the heady days of the railway mania of the 1840s over they were settling into the daily business of transporting people and goods. By the early 1860s the main line from Glasgow to Edinburgh, for example, had been in operation for around fifteen years but the large bridges spanning the Forth and the Tay were still a good fifteen–thirty years away, while the lines to the Western Highlands were still to be proposed and constructed. It was also by this time that rail travel had become sufficiently commonplace to create a market for Bradshaw's guides.

As a young man George Bradshaw had been apprenticed to an engraver in Manchester in 1820, and after a spell in Belfast he returned to Manchester to set up his own business as an engraver and printer specialising principally in maps. In October 1839 he produced the world's first compilation of railway timetables. Entitled *Bradshaw's Railway Time Tables and Assistant to Railway Travelling*, the slender cloth-bound volume sold for sixpence. By 1840 the title had changed to *Bradshaw's Railway Companion* and the price doubled to one shilling. It then evolved into a monthly publication with the price reduced to the original and more affordable sixpence.

Although George Bradshaw died in 1853 the company continued to produce the monthly guides and in 1863 it launched Bradshaw's *Descriptive Railway Hand-Book of Great Britain and Ireland* (which forms the basis of this series of books). It was originally published in four sections as proper guidebooks without any of the timetable information of the monthly publications. Universally referred to as Bradshaw's Guide it was this guidebook that features in Michael Portillo's *Great British Railway Journeys*, and as a result of its exposure to a new audience the book found itself catapulted into the best-seller list almost 150 years after it was originally published.

Without a doubt the Bradshaw Guides were invaluable in their time and they provide the modern-day reader with a fascinating insight into the mid-Victorian rail traveller's experience. In 1865 *Punch* had praised Bradshaw's publications, stating that 'seldom has the gigantic intellect of man been employed upon a work of greater utility'. Having said that, the usual facsimile editions available nowadays don't make especially easy reading with their columns of close-set type. There are scarcely any illustrations for a start, and attempts to trace linear journeys from A to B are interrupted by distracting branch line diversions. That's where this volume comes into its own. *Bradshaw's Guide to Scotland's Railways, Part 2,* takes the reader on a continuous journey from the border at Berwick, up the East Coast to Aberdeen and beyond. The illustrations show scenes from Victorian times and they are juxtaposed with photographs of the locations as they are today. The accompanying information provide greater background detail on the sights to be seen, the railways and the many locations along the route.

The railways

In 1863, the major railway amalgamations that took place in Scotland were still two years away. The main five railway lines that would operate into the 1920s (Glasgow & South Western, Caledonian, North British, Great North of Scotland and Highland) were in existence but the Scottish Central, Inverness & Aberdeen, Edinburgh & Glasgow and numerous other independent companies still existed, breaking up the major routes into smaller sections. On the West Coast route to Aberdeen, one would traverse some three or four different companies' lines and the East Coast route was no better, but this time the route was broken by the Firths of Forth and Tay, with ferries operating to Fife from both Granton and Dundee.

The journey begins with the line from Berwick to Edinburgh and the branches from it. This was North British territory and it encompassed the east coast ports of Leith and Granton, the rich agricultural county of Berwickshire and the sishing harbours of East Lothian. Included were the burgeoning resort towns of Dunbar and North Berwick, with their small harbours.

The primarily rural routes of the Borders are covered, with the lines to Galashiesl, Selkirk, Hawick and Peebles all makng an appearance. Of course, the Waverley Route is not forgotten. North into Fife, the railways radiate along the coast, and across the county, to Dunfermline, Newburgh and Perth as well

Above: George Bradshaw.

Right: An advertising poster for the LNER's route via the Forth Bridge.

Below: Scotland was famed for its innovative railways, from the first electric train on the Edinburgh-Glasgow line to the George Bennie railplane at Milngavie.

FORTH BRIDGE

LONDON & NORTH EASTERN RAILWAY OF ENGLAND AND SCOTLAND

THE TRACK OF THE FLYING SCOTSMAN

THE FIRST "BRADSHAW"
A reminiscence of Whitsun Holidays in Ancient Egypt.   From an old-time tabl(e)ature

Above: Punch pokes some gentle fun at the ubiquitous nature of the Bradshaw publications which included timetables and guides or 'hand-books'. Although George Bradshaw had died in 1853, the publications continued to be known by his name.

as St Andrews and Newport. The rail passenger on the East Coast to Aberdeen experienced the world's first train ferry between Granton and Burntisland, while the railways themselves went into the mining heartland of west Fife.

Into Forfarshire, the railway was again in rich farming country, with two main lines north to Aberdeen and a coastal route that served many fishing harbours, giving them access to London markets for their catch. Northwards to Aberdeen, the railways changed yet again in their look, with the many branches into Deeside and rural Aberdeenshire being built primarily for agricultural or tourist traffic. The Great North of Scotland Railway took the traveller north and west of Aberdeen itself, on a route that, by 1863, connected with Inverness and the beginnings of the railways into the Highlands. Enjoy the journey on the railways of 1863.

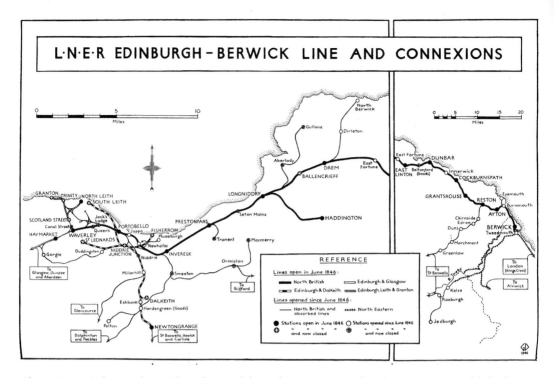

L·N·E·R EDINBURGH – BERWICK LINE AND CONNEXIONS

Above: In 1946, the North British Railway celebrated its centenary. The above map was published for the anniversary in a booklet on the first railway across the border.

Below: An East Coast Route official postcard published by the three main railway lines that operated the line between London Kings Cross and Edinburgh Waverley.

The East Coast Main Line

North British Main Line

BERWICKSHIRE

A maritime county in Scotland, which returns one member. Its extreme length from east to west is 31 miles; many hill forts erected by its former-possessors, the Romans, are still to be seen on the numerous eminences, interspersed with several Roman camps. Indeed the whole county is rich in local antiquities. This county is now divided into Merse, Lammermuir, and Lauderdale. Merse, the southern district, bordering on the Tweed, is very fertile, and when seen from an eminence resembles a vast garden, watered by two tributary streams of the Tweed, called Black and White Waters. Lammermuir, situated to the north of Merse, is a pastoral district, mountainous, hilly, and abounds in game. Lauderdale is situated to the west of the other divisions, and is a mixture of hill and dale. The lower part is very fertile, and like the rest of the county of Berwick.

BERWICK

A telegraph station. Hotels – Red Lion, King's Arms, Salmon.
Market days – Saturday. Fairs – Trinity Friday, second Wednesday in May, Wednesday before 25th August, and first Wednesday in November.
Bankers – Branch of Northumberland and Durham District.

Berwick, or Berwick-on-Tweed, at the Tweed's mouth, is a port, and parliamentary borough, sends two members, and has a population of 13,265, 58 miles from Edinburgh. Before the Union it was an important frontier post, as it commanded the east road, between the two countries. It is still a garrison town, having a military governor, barracks, and fortified walls in the old style; but there are few remains of the castle, that scene of so many contests. Here Edward I crowned his humble servant Balliol, the competitor of Bruce, and barbarously exposed the limbs of the patriot Wallace after his execution. Here, too, he shut up the Countess of Buchan in the infamous wicker cage, for six years. On one occasion, seven Scots took it by surprise, and on another, it was recovered by Henry IV from the Percys (then in rebellion), by the firing of a single shot, which was an entirely new thing to the garrison.

Close to the site of it, is Stephenson's Royal Border Bridge or viaduct, for the railway, 216 ft long, on twenty-eight brick arches, 61 feet span. There is an old one to the Tabart of Tweedmouth, besides

Left: Photographed *c.* 1890, this view shows the original entrance to Berwick Upon Tweed railway station. In May 1846, the railway was passed by the Board of Trade and was ready for opening. The first train left for Berwick on Thursday 18 June 1846. Berwick station was rebuilt in 1927.

Middle: Burnmouth harbour was used by herring boats, which followed the shoals of silvery darlings around the coast.

Below: The locomotive shed at Duns on 18 June 1936 with LNER tank No. 9131 on shed. 9131 had been built for the North British Railway in June 1912 and was of class C15. She was scrapped in 1956 at Kilmarnock works.

the Union Suspension Bridge, some miles up the river, built by Brown, and one of the earliest on this principle. The Town Hall, built in the last century, by Dodd, has a clock tower, 150 feet high. Much of the produce from the interior is shipped here, in the Berwick schooners and clipper ships, but the harbour is full of reefs. About 80 vessels belong to the port – annual customs £15,000. The salmon fisheries in the Tweed, once worth £15,000 a-year, have declined to £4,000. About Christmas, the people here eat kippered salmon and plum-pudding. Salmon is sent to London, packed in ice. Much whisky is exported. It is an exciseable article on the town side of the turnpike gate. Berwick, which is naturally part of Berwickshire, in Scotland, was made independent of both countries, by Henry VIII; latterly it went with Islandshire, an isolated part of Durham; but since the Act of Union, which transferred such portions of counties to that in which they actually stand, it belongs to Northumberland.

Berwick to Edinburgh

Passing Burnmouth station, a place formerly celebrated for smugglers, and near which are some large stone quarries, we reach

AYTON

Distance from station, ½ mile. Telegraph station at Reston Junction, 4 miles.
Hotel – Red Lion.

Passing Reston station, the junction of the

Dunse Branch

We arrive at Chirnside, at which there are paper and flax mills, and in the vicinity Whitehall, seat of Sir J. Hall, Bart, Nineveh, A. Home, Esq., Islington, and Hay of Dunse, where Roman millstones and urns have been found. Fairs at Chirnside, last Thursday in November, for linen and sacking.

Edrom – Here is good trout fishing. In the vicinity are Nisbet, seat of Lord Sinclair, Dunse Spa, Kelloe, G. Buchan, Esq., Kimmeryhawe, R. Bonar, Esq., Allanbank and Blackadder House.

DUNSE

A telegraph station. Hotel – Houram's. Market Days – Saturday.
Fairs – 1st Thursday in June, August, and Nov.

This place, with a population of about 3,162, employed as weavers, contains two chapels, Town Hall, by Gillespie, in the pointed style, in which is a portrait of Duns Scotus, born at Grueldykes Farm in 1274. At

Dunse Law, 630 feet high, Leslie resisted the episcopacy of Charles I, in 1639. Dunse Castle, rebuilt on the site of Lord Randolph's seat, has portraits of the Setons, and commands fine views. Boston and Dr M'Crie were natives. In September, 1790, a Hoopoe was killed here. It is a meet for the Berwick Hunt.

GRANT'S HOUSE

A telegraph station.

On the Eye Water, on the wild hilly slope of the Lammermuir hills, which terminate at the coast on the right in St Abb's Head and Fast Castle – the latter on a point usually identified as the Wolfs Crag of the Master of Ravenswood, in the Bride of Lammermuir. The slate cliffs here are 300 feet high, and pass after a time into the primitive basalt formation. A little beyond Grant's House is the deep pass of Peas Bridge.

COCKBURNSPATH

A telegraph station.

So called after a resident named Coldbrandspath. Close at hand is Dunglas, the seat of Sir J. Hall Bart., the old seat of the Homes and Douglases, which was visited by James VI in 1603 and 1617. Over the Peath there is a bridge built in 1786, about 123 feet high and 300 long, near to which is Fast Castle and the remains of camps, the original of Sir W. Scott's 'Master of Ravenswood.'

Innerwick – This place contains ruins of the Hamiltons' castle, destroyed by Protector Somerset in 1547, and close at hand lies Edinken's Bridge, with the tumuli, on the spot where King Edwin of Northumbria was killed, Black Castle Camp, and an old chapel.

HADDINGTONSHIRE, OR EAST LOTHIAN

Which is situated on the east coast of Scotland, at the mouth of the Firth of Forth, returns one member. The southern part of this county consists of a range of lofty mountains, which formed in ancient times a barrier for the defence of the county, and of the Scottish capital, against the invasions of the English. This elevated district overlooks towards the north and north-east a fertile peninsula, descending gradually to the sea on the north and west, and which in every part exhibits marks of the most successful industry. These mountains are called the Lammermuir Hills, and form part or brunch of a great range which crosses the whole island. A great portion of this county, or at least of the western part of it, from the borders of Lammermuir to the sea, rests upon a bed of the most valuable mineral strata; lime, coal, ironstone, and freestone, everywhere abound.

No county is, perhaps, embellished with a greater number of gentlemen's seats, all of them elegant and well situated, and some built in a style of great magnificence.

DUNBAR

A telegraph station. Hotel – Cossar's.
Market Day – Tuesday. Fairs – Tuesday after May 26th and Nov. 22nd.

A royal burgh and seaport town. It is situated at the mouth of the Firth of Forth, on a gentle eminence. The appearance of the country around, in every direction, presents a variety of striking and picturesque objects. To the cast is seen St Abb's Head, with its bold and rocky coast; to the south are the hills which border upon Lammermuir; westward Dumpenderlaw and North Berwick, and on the north the Firth of Forth, Bass Rock, and the coast of Fife.

Many vestiges of Dunbar Castle yet remain, which give a wild and picturesque effect to the rocks on which they stand. Here a celebrated battle was fought in 1276, in which Lord Warren defeated the Scots, and Cromwell routed Leslie in 1650. Mary Queen of Scots resided in the castle after Rizzio's death. The town contains baths, library, assembly rooms, foundries, grammar school, mathematical school, at which navigation is taught. The church, which is cruciform, was rebuilt in 1819 on the site of the old one founded in 1176 by the Earl of March. Here are tombs as old as 1480, and a fine one of the Lord Treasurer Home. The Rocky Pier has a dry dock, quay, and batteries, it was repaired by Cromwell, and has latterly been improved at a cost of £15,000. It commands views of the Bass, May Island, Forfar, etc. Here General Cope landed in 1745, and Paul Jones anchored. The late Emperor Nicholas of Russia visited it in 1814. Close at hand are Dunbar house, seat of the Earl of Lauderdale – Lochend, Sir G. Warrender, Bart., Ninewar, J. Hamilton, Esq., and Belton, Captain Hay, R.N.

Passing Linton, East Fortune, and DREM stations – junction of the

North Berwick Branch

We reach Dirleton station, near which is the castle taken by Edward I, and now the seat of Mrs Ferguson.

NORTH BERWICK

Telegraph station at Drem, 4¾ miles. Hotel – Dalrymple Arms.

This place contains ruins of a nunnery, founded in 1154 by the Earl of Fife. The port is a very bad rocky tidal harbour, and has a small pier. The rocks of Craigleith and Bass can be seen. In the vicinity is North Berwick House, seat of Sir H. Dalrymple, Bart.

Above, left: Grantshouse Post Office in 1908.

Above, right: Barnsness lighthouse, near Dunbar. The coast here was tricky, with numerous cliffs and reefs, which were a danger to shipping.

Left: Haddington station in 1946. Haddington was the birthplace of John Knox, the Scottish religious reformer.

Below: East Fortune signal box c. 1910.

LONGNIDDRY (Junction)
A telegraph station.

Near at hand, is the old ruined seat at which John Knox was tutor.

HADDINGTON (Branch)
A telegraph station. Hotels – George, Star. Market Day – Friday.
Fairs – Friday after Rutherglen, 2nd Tuesday in July, July 15th, Friday before
Edinbro' Hallow fair. Bankers – Branch of British Linen Co.; Branch of Bank of
Scotland.

Haddington is the capital of the county bearing the same name. It stands
on the left bank of the Tyne, and consists of four principal streets, with
several smaller ones branching from it. Within the last twenty years
this town has been greatly improved. One of its most elegant buildings
is the church, formerly a Franciscan monastery. The suburb of Nungate
is connected by a bridge of three arches across the Tyne. Being situated
in the heart of a rich agricultural district, Haddington is an important
place for the sale and purchase of grain in the open market. It contains
a population of about 3,883, who return one member; two churches,
the oldest of which dating as far hack as Edward I, has a ruined choir,
with tombs of Rev. John Brown, Maitlands, and Blantyres; five chapels;
county-hall, with spire 150 feet high; town-hall, by Adams; School of Art,
founded in 1820; museum, Gray's Public Library, brewery, tanneries, corn
mill, four-arched bridge, grammar school, and dispensary. Here the Earl of
Athol was murdered, in 1242. Knox was born, in 1505, in Gifford Street.
Andrew Maitland, who married in 1657, had nine children, whose ages
counted 738 years. Here prevails the custom of the bellman going round
every night, singing the following:

> A' gold men's servants, whoe'er ye he,
> Keep coal and can'el for charitie, etc.

In the vicinity are Colstoun, the seat of the Marquis of Dalhousie;
Annsfield, Earl Wemyss (on the site of which stood a woollen factory in
Cromwell's time); Cleckington, Sir R. Houston, Bart.; and Stevenson, Sir
J. Sinclair, Bart.

Left: Lammer Law in the Lammermuir Hills. The cairn denotes the top of the hill and the views on a clear day can be spectacular.

Below: The three harbours of Prestonpans, Port Seton and Cockenzie once supported a major fleet of fishing boats. Here, fishermen prepare their tackle at Cockenzie in 1910.

Left: Johnnie Cope's House, Cockenzie. It was here that Sir John Cope stayed before the Battle of Prestonpans. His forces were soundly defeated by the Jacobites and he was last seen heading back to Berwick as fast as he could.

EDINBURGHSHIRE, OR MID-LOTHIAN

The principal part of this county, which returns one member, is mountainous. To the eastward of Edinburgh the country is agreeably variegated, by being formed, at the distance of every two or three miles, into ridges, in a direction from south to north, the whole of which are well cultivated. Each ridge, proceeding to the east, is more lofty than the former, till it terminates in the hills of Lammermoor. Towards the north, that is, upon the coast, the face of the country is rich and beautiful; but on receding from the sea, it gradually loses that aspect, and the mountains are bleak, naked, and barren on the south and south-west. The rivers belonging to this county are of no importance from their magnitude, but they are rendered interesting by the beautiful scenery exhibited almost everywhere upon their steep woody banks. The North and South Esk have beautiful wooded banks, adorned with splendid villas of the nobility or gentry. It rises on the southern side of the Pentland Hills, above Newhall, about 14 miles from Edinburgh, and its banks are not only uncommonly romantic and beautiful, but they form a species of classic ground. The eastern division of this county contains one of the most extensive and rich fields of coal that is anywhere to be found; but notwithstanding the abundance of the coal, the seams being of great thickness, the mines have generally proved unprofitable, in consequence of the enormous expense of working them, from the seams running to great depths. The maritime traffic of the county, which is very considerable, is concentrated in Leith, which possesses the best port in the county. The navigable canal and various lines of railway proceeding from Edinburgh to the rest of Scotland, makes the capital of this county the entrepôt of import as well as of export goods.

PRESTONPANS

A telegraph station.

This place was celebrated for the battle of that name, between Prince Charles Stuart and the Royalists under Sir John Cope, in which the latter was defeated, Sept. 21st, 1745. In its neighbourhood is Tranent, with its Church, rebuilt in 1838, containing the tomb of Col. Gardiner, who fell at the battle of Prestonpans. In the vicinity is Seton House, rebuilt by Adam in 1790, on the old site close to the Collegiate Church, and Falside Castle, the Seton's seat, which was captured by Somerset on the day of Pinkie Battle.

We then reach Inveresk, (a telegraph station) beautifully situated in a healthy spot above the Firth of Forth, close to Pinkey, where the Scots were defeated in 1547, and Carberry Hill, 540 feet high; Fullerton's seat, where Mary surrendered to Kirkcaldy of Grange, and which was occupied by Cromwell, and by the Highlanders in 1745. In the Church, which has

17

A TASTY DISH - MUSSELS !! FROM MUSSELBURGH

Left: Musselburgh is named after the shellfish commonly found in the seas around. Here, fishwives sell the freshly caught catch on the roadside in, where else, but Musselburgh!

Middle: Fisherrow harbour in the 1950s.

Below: Portobello pier was once the grand centrepiece of the Victorian resort. The close proximity to Edinburgh saw many thousands visit Portobello every weekend in the summer. From the traditional donkeys to the Marine Gardens, and all the fun of the fair, you could see and do everything in Portobello. The chain pier was built in 1821 and was one of the oldest piers in Britain. Sadly, it was extensively damaged at the end of the nineteenth century and removed. A new pier, shown here, was built in the 1870s, designed by Sir Thomas Bouch, who also designed the first Tay Bridge. It was demolished between the wars.

FISHERROW FROM THE HARBOUR, MUSSELBURGH

been rebuilt, was found, in 1565, an altar to Apollo, coins, bust, etc. Close at hand is Cromwell's Fort, remains of Loretto Chapel, New Hailes, Sir J. Ferguson, Bart.; Edmonstone, J. Wauchope, Esq.; and Wallyford, A. Finlay, Esq.

MUSSELBURGH

A telegraph station. Hotel – Musselburgh Arms.

Market day – Friday. Fair – 2nd Tuesday in October.

This burgh and bathing place contains a fine church, five chapels, library, bathing establishments, masonic lodge, on the site of which Randolph died in 1322, Grammar School, Lunatic Asylum, Sailors' Society, founded in 1669. An old bridge with a drawbridge in the middle, and Rennie's five-arched bridge. In the vicinity are Pinkie House, Sir J. Hope, Bart,, Fisherow, a Roman station. Sheriff Hall, with its remains of a camp, the Links, on which in 1774, a golf club played for a silver cup, Huntley met the Covenanters in 1638, Cromwell encamped in 1650, and where the Edinburgh races are held. J. Burnet, the engraver, and Ritchie, the sculptor, are natives.

Passing New Hailes and Niddrie, near which is Niddrie Marechal, seat of A. Wauchope, Esq., whose ancestors in 1389 founded a small chapel here, we proceed to JOPPA, at which are a mineral spring, quarry, and saltworks, and arrive at Portobello.

PORTOBELLO

Telegraph station at Edinburgh, 3 miles.

Hotels: Commercial; Crown.

This place has gradually increased since a sailor, who was at the capture of Porto Bello in 1739, built a residence here; it now contains six chapels, bank, baths, Union Hall, glass, soap, brick, and pottery works, paper mill, and various schools. It is one of the principal watering places on the east coast of Scotland. In 1822 George the Fourth held a review on the sands, which extend about a mile in length. Fishwives' Causeway, leading to Edinburgh an old Roman road.

LEITH

A telegraph station. Hotels: Old Ship, 28, Shore; New Ship, 20 Shore; Globe, 23, Sandfort Street. Omnibuses to and from Edinburgh every five minutes, from 9 a.m. until 10 p.m. Steamers: See Edinburgh. Races in July.

Bankers: Branch of Bank of Scotland; Branch of British Linen Co.; Branch of Commercial Bank of Scotland; Branch of National Bank of Scotland; Branch of Royal Bank of Scotland.

This port to the city of Edinburgh returns one member along with the burghs of Portobello and Musselburgh. It was formerly called Inverleith, and is built on the river Leith, from which it derives its name; it was frequently plundered, the shipping burned, and the pier destroyed by the English, from 1313 to 1544. About four years after, during the minority of Queen Mary, it was fortified by a French General, who came over to suppress the Reformation. Queen Mary landed here from France in 1541. In 1650 Cromwell occupied the town, and exacted an assessment from the inhabitants ; after his return to England the citadel was built, which was taken in 1715 by some of the Stuart family, and held for a short time; in 1822 George IV landed. There are about twenty churches, among which may be mentioned the parish church of South Leith, a Gothic edifice supposed to have been built in the 15th century. John Home, author of Douglas, is interred here. It contains Court House, Town Hall, Police Office, Post Office, Exchange Buildings, Chamber of Commerce, Assembly Rooms, Reading Rooms, Libraries, Schools, Hospital, Infirmary, Trinity House, rebuilt in 1817 on the site of the old one built by Queen Mary (whose portrait, by Mytens is contained). Custom House, built in 1812, at a cost of £12,000. Docks, Bonded Warehouses, Harbour, and two beautiful piers extending on each side of the harbour to about a mile in length, making a delightful promenade.

EDINBURGH

Telegraph station at 68, Princes Street, and at the Parliament House.
Hotels – McGregor's Royal, first-class, for families and gentlemen, in Princes Street; Murray's London, family and commercial, St Andrew's Square; Mackay's, for families and gentlemen; Barry's British, for families and gentlemen; Douglas's, for families and gentlemen; Rampling's Waterloo.
New Rooms – Harthill's, 23, Waterloo Place; Robertson and Scott, 7(1, George Street. Tariff – Id. per visit).
Omnibuses – to and from the stations and Leith every five minutes.
Steamers from Granton Pier and Leith Harbour; Edinburgh offices for Aberdeen and Inverness at 6, South St Andrew Street; General Steam Navigation Co., for London, 21, Waterloo Place; Leith and Edinburgh Co., for London, 9, Waterloo Place; Stirling, 10, Princes Street.
Market Days – Wednesday, vegetable and fruit market; Tuesday, Thursday, and Saturday.
Post Office at Waterloo Place.

This city, which has not unaptly been termed the 'modern Athens', is one of the most ancient in this country. Its schools for the acquirement of useful knowledge have long held a high rank amongst the universities of Europe, and have supplied some of the most distinguished statesmen, warriors, poets, and divines, who have graced our annals.

It contains beauties and peculiarities which give it a high claim to attention amongst the capitals of Europe, and is the capital of Scotland in a superb situation on the north slope of the Pentland Hills, fronting the Firth of Forth, two miles from it. Two members returned.

Edinburgh, So called from Edwin, king of Northumbria, who built a castle here in the seventh century, while others claim the origin from the two Gaelic words, 'Dun Edin', which signifies 'the face of a hill'. It covers a space of from two to two-and-a-half miles square, and contains the old town on the cast between the Castle, Holyrood Palace, and the Abbey; the south town, round Heriot's Hospital, Newington, and Morningside; and the new town on the north and north-west. Both the south and new towns have been erected within the last hundred years; the latter especially, comprises many noble streets and squares, built of the beautiful stone from Craigleith quarry (two miles distant from the city). In the old town, along the High Street, Canongate, Grassmarket, etc., many houses are of Queen Mary's time, divided by narrow dark closes (or alleys), and from six to ten stories (or flats) high. Between it and the new town are east and west Princes Street Gardens, beautifully laid out, and through which the Edinburgh & Glasgow, and North British railways pass: this was formerly called the North or Nor' Loch, a sheet of stagnant water; there are the North and Waverley bridges, and Mound, forming a connection with the old and new town. Of the numerous fine structures which adorn the 'Modern Atheus', as it has been styled from a similarity in its general appearance, the

Castle on a Hill, 383 feet above the level of the sea, is surmounted by modern batteries, the state prison and arsenal, Queen Mary's room (where she gave birth to James VI), the regalia room (admittance free by order from City Chambers); among the regalia are Bruce's Crown and Sceptre. Mons Meg, a large cannon, said to be cast at Mons, in Brittany, in 1486, is mounted on a carriage on the Bomb Battery. The Queen and Prince Albert ascended it for the view in 1842. The castle ought to be visited an account of the magnificent prospect it affords; on the north side of the castle esplanade is a statue to the Duke of York. College of Justice, in Parliament Square, where the thirteen judges sit, where are statues of President Forbes, Blair, Lord Melville, Dundas, and the late Lord Jeffrey; adjoining is the Advocates' Library, containing nearly 200,000 printed volumes, and 1,700 manuscripts. Among the MSS. is a Bible of the 11th century, and the original Solemn League and Covenant. Signet Library is peculiarly rich in the department of History, especially British and Irish. In the centre of the square is a Statue of Charles II, on horseback. General Post Office, in Waterloo Place, a Grecian building. Stamp and Excise Offices, in Waterloo Place. General Register House, Princes Street (foot of North Bridge), a handsome Grecian pile, with a tower 200 feet high; immediately in front is the Equestrian Statue of the Duke of Wellington, by Steel.

Edinburgh

Above, left: Princes Street, Edinburgh, and the Castle in the 1890s. By this time Waverley Station had been rebuilt.

Above, right: The original signal box from the 1840s, at Waverley Station. This controlled the southern approaches to the station.

Left: The rebuilding of Waverley Station in the 1890s. Two North Eastern Railway locomotives are in the foreground.

Bottom left: Holyrood House, home of the Royal Family in Edinburgh, with the builders in, repairing the roadways in front of the royal palace.

Nelson's Monument, on Calton Hill, 102 feet in height – on the top is a Time Ball, which is lowered at one o'clock, Greenwich time. National Monument, on Calton Hill, unfinished, consists of twelve great pillars, and erected at a cost of £13,000; it is a model of the Parthenon of Athens. Close by are monuments to Dugald Stewart and Professor Playfair, and the Royal Observatory, shaped like a St George's Cross, 62 feet long. Scott's Monument, in East Princes Street Gardens, one of the finest ornaments of Edinburgh, is shaped like a pyramid, 200 feet high, from the designs of G. Kemp (a self-taught architect), with niches for statues illustrative of characters in the works of Scott. Only five have been filled. A Statue of Scott, by Steel, is placed underneath. Royal Institution, on the Mound, founded in 1810, a handsome Grecian portico, with Steel's statue of Queen Victoria in front, contains a gallery of casts (open every day, except Saturday), and a line gallery of paintings (open Wednesday and Saturday, free); here are held the meetings of the Society of Arts, Royal Society, and Society of Antiquarians, offices of the Board of Trade for Manufactures, and Board of Fisheries in Scotland. National Gallery, behind the Royal Institution, lately completed, was built for the annual exhibitions of the Royal Scottish Academy, the School of Design, and the institution of a Scottish National Gallery of paintings and sculpture. University, on South Bridge, founded in 1582, by a charter from James VI, the present building was begun in 1789, by Robert Adams; there are thirty-two professorships, divided into four faculties, viz.: Medicine, Law, Theology, and Arts; a Museum open daily, 6d. (Saturday free), and Library, 198 feet in length, containing about 100,000 volumes. Royal College of Surgeons' Museum, in Neilson Street, admittance by member's order. John Knox's House, foot of High Street, open on Tuesdays, Fridays, and Saturdays (6d), consists of three rooms, the principal object being the chair which belonged to the Reformer. The Canongate, containing many houses of note, extends from the foot of High Street to Holyrood Palace. In this street is situated the White Horse Inn, at which Dr Samuel Johnson arrived on his way to the Hebrides in 1773; Moray House, on the south of the street, was erected in 1618 or 1623. Here Oliver Cromwell took up his residence on his first visit to Edinburgh, 1618.

Holyrood Palace (open daily, 6d., Saturday, free) and Abbey, the latter being founded for Augustine Canons, by David I, in 1128; the present palace is for the most part a building about 200 years old, here Queen Mary was married to Darnley, in 1565; the Gothic tower, doorways, and Chapel Royal, still remain. The palace, which has been partially restored for the Queen, contains a quadrangle in the style of Hampton Court. Queen Mary's bedroom and cabinet, with the mark (?) of David Rizzio's blood; in the picture gallery there are about 110 manufactured likenesses of Scottish sovereigns, principally executed by De Witt, a Flemish painter. Queen Mary's Dial is in the gardens. Arthur's Seat, in the park behind, 822 feet above the level of the sea, is surrounded by a fine carriage-way called the 'Queen's Drive'; on the north side is the ruins of a chapel dedicated to St. Anthony the Eremite. Salisbury Crags (forming part of Arthur's Seat), is a range of precipitous rocks, and from the road winding round the foot may be seen the cottage of 'Davie Deans', rendered famous by Scott's celebrated novel, the Heart of Mid-Lothian; in this work is to he had the best description of old Edinburgh.

City and Commercial buildings. Edinburgh is governed by a Lord Provost, six Magistrates or Bailies, and Councillors. Bailie Court and Council Chambers are in the Old Exchange Buildings, High Street; nearly opposite is the Police Office, in front of which is the spot where formerly stood the City Cross, removed in 1756. County Hall, Parliament Square, occupied as offices for the Sheriff and Procurator Fiscal; the Small Debt Courts are held here; between it and St Giles' Church formerly stood the famous 'Old Tolbooth Prison', or heart of Mid-Lothian, the scene of the Porteus riots. Its gate is now at Abbotsford. Corn Exchange, in the Grassmarket, a handsome Italian building, 156 feet long. Commercial Bank (George Street) and British Linen Company's Bank (St Andrew's Square); the interior of which are well worth a visit. County Jail, in Waterloo Place, was completed in 1847, and has accommodation for criminal and debtor prisoners. Water Works, on the Castle Hill, capable of containing 1,800,000 gallons of water, and filled by pipes about 8 miles long, from the vale of Glencarse, in the Pentland Hills.

Places of amusements, etc. Horticultural Society Gardens, Inverleith Row, admitted by a member's order; close to are the Royal Botanic Gardens, open daily, free. Zoological Gardens, at Claremont Crescent, open daily, 1s. Antiquarian Museum, 24, George Street (Wednesday and Saturday, by member's order). Here are preserved many interesting relics of antiquity. Highland and Agricultural Society Museum, George IV Bridge, every day, except Monday, free; Royal and Queen's Theatres, Waterloo Rooms, Music Hall, Hopetown Rooms, St. Cecilia Hall, and Queen Street Hall, used principally for lectures and concerts. Short's Observatory, on Castle Hill, containing many fine astronomical instruments.

Public cemeteries and churchyards. Greyfriars – here Mackenzie, 'the Man of Feeling', is buried, etc. Warresten, near Inverleith Row; Western or Dean, where Francis Jeffrey, and Wilson, 'The Christopher North', of Blackwood's Magazine, are buried; Southern Grange, Dr. Chalmers is buried here.

Churches and Chapels. There are about 100 places of worship, about thirty of which belong to the Established Church. Three churches are comprised under the roof of St Giles', in the form of a cross, 206 feet long, of the 14th century, with a spire 160 feet high, and musical bells; John Knox, the Regent Murray, and Montrose, are buried here. Victoria or Assembly Hall, with a spire 240 feet high. Here the General Assembly of the Church of Scotland meets in May. Old Greyfriars Church, built in 1612, destroyed by fire in 1845, and now in course of rebuilding. Uniform with it is the New Greyfriars, with which it is contiguous. Tron Church, High Street, marked by a new spire of 140 feet. The church was built in 1663; here Chalmers preached. Opposite the church is a cellar where the Treaty of Union is said to have been signed. St Andrew's, in George Street, with spire 168 feet. In St Andrew's Square, at the east end of this fine street, is the Melville Pillar, copied from Trajan's; in the square Lord Brougham was born. In a line with Melville in George Street, are statues of Pitt and George IV. St. George's, at the west end of this street in Charlotte Square, with flue portico and dome, 15 feet high, after the model of St Paul's. St Stephen's St Vincent Street, a fine building, with, a tower, 162 feet high. St Cuthbert's or West Church, Princes Street, is a large church, the mother church to a number of chapels of ease. Canongate, in the form of a cross, finished in 1683, with figures of the deer and cross on it, which is said to have appeared to David I, and led him to found Holyrood. Smith, author of the Wealth of Nations, and Ferguson, the poet, are buried hero, St John's Episcopal Chapel, Princes Street, is In the Gothic style, built in 1818. St Paul's Episcopal Chapel (the Bishop officiates here), in York Place, a Gothic building. St Mary's Roman Catholic Chapel, in Broughton Place, built 1813, is the principal place of worship of that body in Edinburgh, has a fine organ, and a painting, by Vandyke, of the Entombment. Trinity Episcopal Church, at the Dean Bridge; St Mary's, belonging to the Established Church, in Belle Vue Crescent, with a spire 180 feet high, and opened in 1824; John Knox Church close to the Reformer's house. Free Church College, a modem building, erected shortly after the disruption.

Schools, Hospitals and benevolent Institutions. The public and private schools exceed 200 and the benevolent and religious societies are very numerous. The High School, Calton Hill, dates as far back as 1517, was rebuilt on its present site in 1820. Edinburgh Academy, Henderson Row, built in 1824; Naval and Military Academy, in Lothian Road; Normal School, for the training of pupil teachers, is at the back of the Castle. Heriot's Hospital, in Laurieston, is an Elizabethan quadrangle, by Inigo Jones, 160 feet square; Heriot is 'Jingling Geordie', in the Fortunes of Nigel, by Scott. George Watson's Hospital, in Laurieston; John Watson's Hospital, at the Dean, in the Grecian style of building; Gardner's Orphan Hospital, at the Dean, opposite Watson's; Stewart's Hospital, close to the two last mentioned, is built in the Elizabethan style; Merchant Maiden's Institution, to the west of George Watson's; Trade's Maiden Hospital, in the Meadows. These hospitals are all for the training and education of children of both sexes. Gillespie's Hospital, Bruntsfield Links, for the aged and infirm. This is the only hospital of the kind in Edinburgh. Lunatic Hospital, Morningside; Royal Infirmary, is a large building close to the University, and supported by subscriptions. There are many other

Left: A view of part of Edinburgh's medieval Old Town in 1870. Shown here are the Tolbooth and Canongate on the Royal Mile.

Below: A feature of Edinburgh life for decades has been the Highland Show, held in Ingliston. It's still the premier agrcultural show in Scotland.

excellent charitable institutions, maintained by private subscriptions – among them may be mentioned the House of Refuge, Blind Asylum, Night Asylum for the Houseless, Deaf and Dumb Institution, Destitute Sick Society, two Ragged Schools, Public Dispensaries, etc.

In George Square, near the Meadows, Sir Walter Scott was born, in 1771. Allan Ramsay's House, on Castlehill. A small stream, called the 'Water of Leith', runs through the new town to the sea at Leith, passing the Dean and two other bridges. The Dean bridge is a very fine one, by Telford, in four arches, spanning a deep ravine, 106 feet high from the bed of the stream, and commanding an extensive view. Three or four unhappy creatures have leaped over. A short distance to the east of Dean Bridge, on the right side of the stream, is St Bernard's Mineral Well, and much frequented by invalids and others. Bruntsfield Links, a famous place for the game of golf; near to it is Merchieston Castle, the birth place of Napier, the inventor of Logarithms. It is now used as an educational institution.

Above: Edinburgh Castle, an important stronghold since medieval times, is built on one of Edinburgh's extinct volcanoes. Arthur's Seat is another. Perched high above the Commonwealth Pool, its summit was once the haunt of itinerant tradesmen selling lemonade and snacks to thirsty walkers.

Above: The headquarters of the Coldstream Guards.

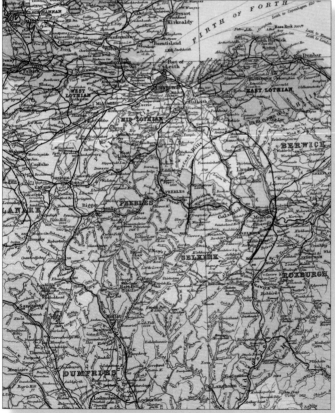

Left: Map showing the Borders railways in the 1920s.

The Waverley Route & Border Branches

The Borders Branches
Kelso, Tweedmouth, and Hawick Branches

Berwick to Kelso and Roxburgh

This line runs along the south bank of the Tweed. Passing Halidon Hill, where the Scotch were defeated by Edward III, we very soon arrive at the station of

NORHAM

Telegraph station at Tweedmouth, 6¾ miles.

Here is a very old church and a border castle, the ruins of which are approached by means of a suspension bridge across the river. It is thus referred to by Sir Walter Scott, in his Marmion:

Day sets on Norham's castled steep,
And Tweed's fair river, broad and deep,
And Cheviot's mountains lone.

The tide flows to this point; Twizel Castle, seat of Sir F. Blake, Bart., on the 'sullen Till', which
fails in hero, near the old Gothic bridge, which Surrey crossed on the way to Flodden Field.

High sight it is and haughty, while
They dive into the deep defile
Beneath the castles airy wall.

The present castle is modern.

CORNHILL, (for Coldstream)

Telegraph station at Tweedmouth, 12¼ miles. Hotel – Railway.
Fair – December 6th.

Close at hand is Flodden Field, noted for the battle fought between James IV. of Scotland and the Earl of Surrey, in 1513, in which the former was defeated and slain. Near the church is a mineral spring, and traces of a castle taken by the Scots in 1549.

Left: North British Railway 0-6-2T No. 863 was an NBR Class A tank loco, as much at home as a pilot engine on the Cowlairs incline as it was on a branch line out of Carlisle or Edinburgh.

Above: Floors Castle, near Kelso, *c.* 1900. This is the seat of the Duke of Roxburghe and was built by William Adam in the 1720s.

Left: A Sentinel steam shunter is steaming up outside Kelso's North British locomotive shed in 1936.

Coldstream stands opposite an old ford of the river, and being on Scottish ground, it has become, like Gretna Green, a place for runaway matches – Lord Brougham's, for instance. Here Monk waited his time to declare for Charles II, with some veterans who formed the earliest regiment of the Coldstream Guards. Lees, seat of Sir J. Marjoribanks, Bart.

Wark station.

ROXBURGHSHIRE, or TEVIOTDALE

The western portion of this county is very mountainous, and in the greatest part of its length its southern boundary is also mountainous, adjoining the great ridge called the Cheviot Hills, which, in the upper or western part of Roxburghshire, stretch northward into Scotland. Its external appearance is, upon the whole, extremely beautiful, containing a succession of hills and dales, through which a great number of small rivers take their course along deep and winding valleys. The county is divided into four districts, and returns one member. The most westerly and mountainous part of it is called Hawick; the second or middle district, which is farther down the county towards the east, Jedburgh; the third and lowest district, occupying the eastern part of the county on both sides of the Tweed, Kelso; the fourth and last, Melrose, and is formed of that portion of the county which is situated to the northward of the rest.

CARHAM

Telegraph station at Kelso, 4½ miles.

Close at hand are the lone green round-headed Cheviot Mountains, and Carham Castle – another celebrated border fortress. There is good fishing in the river, and fine views from Skiddaw, one of the Cheviot Hills, to the south, where the highest peak rises 2,600 feet high. The famous border fight of Chevy Chase, or Otterburn, took place in one of its passes, in 1338. After leaving Carham, we now cross the March Burn, and enter Scotland, soon after which we arrive at

Sprouston, near which is a fall of 40 feet, at Newton Don, on the Eden, the seat of R. Balfour, Esq. At Ednam Manse, the poet Thomson was born in 1700; Sitchell, the old seat of the Homes, on a hill, 900 feet high.

KELSO

A telegraph station. Homes – Cross Keys, and Queen's Head. Market Day – Friday. Races in spring and autumn. Fairs – Monthly, and second Friday in May, 6th July, August, and 2nd November.

Kelso is a market town (population about 4,788) in Scotland, which stands on the north side of the Tweed, opposite the junction of that river with the Teviot. It may be considered as the provincial capital of the surrounding fertile country, and noted for its manufacture of woollen tweeds, etc. Its inhabitants are polished,

Above: Roxburgh Castle was destroyed by the Scots in 1460 and is located in the grounds of Floors Castle.

Left: The Kelso NBR engine shed.

Bottom left: Smailholm Tower is a well-preserved fifteenth-century fortified towerhouse. Once home to the Pringles and Scotts, it provided inspiration for local author Sir Walter Scott, who is buried at nearby Dryburgh.

well-informcd, and live in a style of considerable elegance, or rather luxury. The situation of the town is uncommonly beautiful. It stands on the bank of a noble river, at the foot of that fertile tract of country which descends gradually from the heights of Lammermuir, and terminates on the borders of the Tweed. Here Scott's Border Minstrelsy was first published by Ballantyne, and in 1800 Rennie erected a noble five-arched bridge.

Nothing can be more beautiful than the scenery in this neighbourhood, when viewed from an eminence called Pinnacle Hill, on the southern bank of the river, from whence the country is seen to great advantage. The town lies in front, in a low valley. Immediately round it the country rises as if formed into terraces; cultivated fields, woods, and country seats, gradually ascend above each other, to the distance northwards of twelve or fourteen miles, forming an extensive landscape, which in richness and variety is scarcely to be equalled in Scotland.

The principal ornament of Kelso is its ancient abbey, founded by David I, and public library, the former of which suffered considerable damage during the Reformation, but was subsequently converted into a Protestant church. Close at hand are Fleurs Castle, the fine modem Gothic seat of the Duke of Roxburgh, and Springwood, Sir W. Douglas, Bart.

ROXBURGH (North British)
Population, about 1,141. A telegraph station.

This place was formerly the capital of the county. The moat of the castle still remains. Kings Alexander II and III were married here in great pomp. Close to a holly in the river, James II was killed by the bursting of a cannon, in 1460. Good purple trout abound in the streams. In the vicinity are Makerstoun, the fine country seat of Sir T, Brisbane, Bart., and Smailholm Tower, 'the scene of one of Scott's ballads, and the frequent resort of his grandfather.'

Jedburgh Branch
From Roxburgh Junction we turn to the left, and pass the stations of Old Ormiston, Nisbet and Jedfoot Bridge, and soon arrive at

JEDBURGH
A telegraph station. Hotels – Spread Eagle, The Commercial, and The Harrow. Market Days – Thursday and Saturday. Fairs – Monthly.

This place contains the ruins of an abbey older than 1,000, rebuilt by David I. Here Alexander III was married, at which ceremony it is reported that a masque dressed as Death appeared, and Mary Queen of Scots fell ill after her visit to Hermitage Castle to meet Bothwell. The Church is part of that which belonged to the old abbey, having the ancient tower (100 feet), Norman door, nave, etc. Grey Friars was built in 1513. There Bell wrote his 'Rota Temporum', and the Relief Synod began here in 1765. The tower where Queen Mary stayed, is in an ancient

Sir Walter Scott was an advocate, judge and legal administrator but he is best known for his writing. He died in 1832 and is buried at Dryburgh Abbey. It was Scott who encouraged George IV to visit Scotland and managed the royal visit, making elements of Scottish tradition acceptable again, including the use of tartan and the modern-day Highland dress.

street. Caves are to be seen at Hunderlee and Linthaughlee Camp. Thomson and Rutherford were educated at the Grammar School. Sir David Brewster and Mrs Somerville were natives. St Boswell and Dryburgh Abbey are easily accessible from this place.

Passing Rutherford, we soon arrive at

MAXTON

1½ mile (across the suspension bridge, a ford for vehicles) is Mertown, the seat of Lord Polwarth, head of all the Scotts. Here Sir Walter Scott wrote several of his works (amongst others Marmion), and G. P. R. James, the prolific novelist, obtained the materials for his historical romances. To the left of Maxton are Lilliard's Edge, Ancrum Moor, where Archibald 'Bell the Cat' defeated the English in 1544; Mount Teviot, seat of the Marquis of Lothian, close to the Waterloo pillar, from which can be seen Teviotdale and Jedburgh, with its antique abbey church. Not far distant is St Boswell, celebrated for its large July cattle fair. The next station is Newtown, the junction with the main line from Carlisle and Newcastle to the North.

BORDER COUNTIES

Newcastle to Edinburgh – Waverley Route

This line forms the eastern fork to what is called the Waverley route to Edinburgh, and commences at Hexham, on the Newcastle and Carlisle Railway. Nevertheless, arrangements exist by which parties can book direct from Newcastle to Edinburgh and the North, via Perth, The country through which this line traverses for some distance beyond Hawick abounds in limestone, coal, and iron, and is rather wild and moorish in its character. Skirting the eastern banks of the Tyne, almost to its source in the Cheviots, as the railway proceeds northward, the country assumes a highly picturesque diameter, and becomes rich in its historical associations, being immortalised by the pen of Sir Walter Scott.

Wall, so called no doubt from its situation near to the Cilurnum station of the great Hadrian's wall, which intersects our route at this point. Although this wall was constructed some sixteen centuries ago some portions, as well as some of its stations, are still traceable, particularly in this locality.

Wark, Chollerford, Chollerton, Barrasford, and Reedsmouth station.

BELLINGHAM

Telegraph station at Hexham, 17 miles. Market Day – Saturday.

Fairs – May, Saturday before the 12th; September, 1st Wednesday after 15th.

A polling town, situated on the North Tyne, with a population of about 800, principally employed in the mines and quarries, the neighbourhood of which

Above: Langholm Station in 1910. Ubiquitous enamel advertising signs include OXO and Van Houten's Cocoa.

Below: By the 1930s, many small stations were uneconomic. In an effort to keep lines profitable, railcars, such as the Sentinel one shown here at Langholm, were introduced. This one is *Nettle* but there were many others used in Scotland on routes deemed unprofitable.

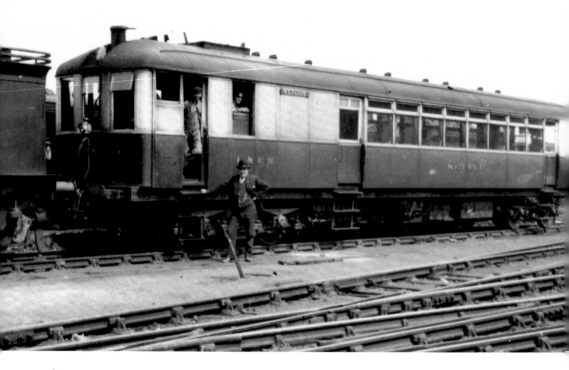

abounds in limestone, coal, and iron. Leaving Bellingham, pass the stations of Tarset, Thorneyburn, Falstone, Plashetts, Kielder and Saughtree, to

Riccarton, the junction with the line from Carlisle.

Border Union
Carlisle to Edinburgh

Leaving the Citadel Station, the next 3 miles brings us beyond Port Carlisle Junction to Harker. Passing onward we arrive quickly at

West Lynton, situated on the south bank of the river Line. The Solway here presents itself to view.

LONGTOWN

Market Days – Monday and Thursday.

This is the junction of short line to Gretna and the Ayrshire lines. The town stands on the east bank of the river Esk, crossed at this point by the railway. It was founded by the Grahams, of Netherby Hall, situated about a mile to the north of the town. Farming improvements have here been made on a large scale.

Scotch Dike station.

Biddings, the junction of the line to Langholm, situated at the confluence of the rivers Esk and Liddel, the latter of which, for the next 8 miles to the base of the Cheviots, forms the boundary line between England and Scotland.

LANGHOLM BRANCH

In a very few moments after leaving the junction, on crossing the Liddel, the traveller is transferred from English to Scottish soil, and he is now in the county of Dumfries. Passing along the side of the Esk, in about seven minutes we are brought to a stand at the small station of

Canobie, the present terminus of the branch. The remainder of the journey is travelled by coach, a distance of 5¾ miles.

LANGHOLM

Market Day – Wednesday.

Situated on the river Esk, here crossed by a bridge. The river furnishes good fishing. The place is supplied with the usual buildings of a chartered town, and its population principally weavers. The country around is of a hilly but fertile character. Traces of Border towers, and some Roman coins, have been found.

Returning to Biddings junction, we again pursue our course, and, passing the small station of Penton, very soon arrive at ...

Cornet's Chase.

Left: The Cornet's Chase, Hawick. This is an annual event commemorating the capture of an English flag in 1514. The event also commemorates the Riding of the Marches, or the boundaries of the burgh.

Lower left: The Cheviots are famed for their wool. An advert postcard from the early twentieth century.

Below: Hawick High Street in the 1890s. What is interesting is the number of children barefoot. Note the group standing around the street vendor's cart on the right-hand side of the image.

KERSHOPE FOOT

Situated at the foot of the porphyry range of hills called the Cheviots. The small stream called the Kershope, which here empties itself into the Liddel, runs along their base, and both together taking a north-easterly direction, form another section of the boundary line between Roxburgh and Cumberland. Immediately on leaving the station we enter the Liddesdale district of the small shire of Roxburgh. With the Liddel in close proximity to our left, we soon approach Newcastletown, a place of some note, on the opposite side of the river. We next pass the station of Steele Road, and in a very few minutes the arrival of the train is announced at

RICCARTON

The point of junction of the Border Union and Border Counties lines with the Waverley route. Soon after leaving this station we enter the district of the Teviotdale, and immediately after passing Shankend we arrive at the station of Stobbs, near to which is the castle of that name, the residence of Sir W. P. Elliot, Bart, and birthplace of General Lord Heathfield.

HAWICK

A telegraph station. Hotels – Tower; Crown. Market Day – Thursday.
Fairs – May 17th, first Thursday after St Boswell's, 1st and 20th September, 3rd Tuesday in October, and November 8th.

This town stands near the confluence of the rivers Teviot and Sletterich, on the great road from Edinburgh to London. It has of late years undergone considerable improvements. The inhabitants chiefly engaged in the woollen, lambswool, and cotton hose trade. It contains on excellent library (4,000 vols.), established in 1762, and Trades' Library, (1,500 vols.), School of Arts, Mechanics' Institute, Farmers' Club (the oldest in Scotland), established in 1770, Nursery, Grammar, and Sunday School (the latter of which was one of the first established in Scotland). The church, which is a fine edifice, is built on the site of that from which Sheriff Ramsay was carried off in 1342, by William Douglas, and contains the books of Orrocks, secretary to the Queen of James VI. In 1500, the rector was Gavin Douglas. Here are remains of Roman and British camps, from which are beautiful prospects. Somerville, the historian of Queen Anne's reign, was a native. In the vicinity are Cavers, seat of J. Douglas, Esq. (here Dr Leyden was born), Briaryard, T. Turnbull, Esq.; Burngrar, W. Watson, Esq.; Midshields, A. Douglas, Esq.; Todrig, G, Pott, Esq.; Sinton, J. Scott, Esq.; Woll, Colonel Scott; Honcot, J. Stuart, Esq.; Chisholm, W. Chisholm, Esq.

Hassendean – Hassendean Burn, the scat of Miss Dickson, is close at hand.
New Velses station.

Above: Langlands Place, Newton St Boswells, 1905. A Roman camp was close by.

Left: Melrose Abbey was founded in 1136 by Cistercian monks but was damaged by the English in 1544. The heart of Robert the Bruce is buried in the Abbey.

Lower left: The locomotive shed at Galashiels on 17 July 1937 with ex-NBR 4-4-0 locomotive No. 9890 on shed. Hidden behind a wagon on the left is a Sentinel railcar.

NEWTOWN

To the left of this place may be seen the Three Eildon Hills, having Trimontium, a Roman camp, on the highest, which is 1,630 feet. Bernerside, the fine old seat of the Haig family, is also near.

At a distance of two miles Dryburgh Abbey may be reached by a beautiful walk along the tortuous Tweed. This ruin was formerly in possession of the Buchan family, who were ejected some years ago; some fantastic modern monuments, which disgraced the owner's taste, have been removed. The ruin is in a good state of preservation, and worth visiting, and may be described in the words of the poet:

> There fifty monks have sang the pray'r
> To God, the King of all;
> There Scott and Lockhart sleep, and wait
> The last great judgment call.

A most magnificent view can be obtained in clear weather from Wallace's statue on the hill.

At St. Boswell's there is a good inn, as also good trout-fishing. It affords great facilities for visitors to Dryburgh, Smailholm, Abbotsford, etc.

MELROSE

A telegraph station. Hotels – The George, Family & Commercial, Thompson's, King's Head.

Coaches to and from New Belses (via Jedburgh rail, fares, 3s., 2s. 3d, and 1s. 6d.), Drygrange, Cowdenknoews, Earlston, and Carrolside, daily.

Flys – [various]. Market Day – Saturday.

Melrose is situated in a fertile vale, at the foot of Eildron Hills, through which flows the Tweed. Outside the town stands Melrose Abbey, founded by david I, one of the most celebrated and magnificent ecclesiastical edifices in Scotland. Even in its present state of decay the pile remains a monument of architectural taste and skill of almost unrivalled beauty. 'The stone,' says Scott, 'though it has resisted the weather for so many ages, retains perfect sharpness, so that even the most minute ornaments seem as entire as when they were wrought. In some of the cloisters there are representations of flowers, vegetables, etc., carved in stone with accuracy and precision so delicate, that we almost distrust our senses.' In the Lay of the Minstrel we have the following graphic description of this splendid ruin:

> Spreading herbs and flow'rets bright
> Glistened with the dew of night;
> Nor herb nor flow'ret glistened there,
> But was carve in the cloister arches fair.

The darkened roof rose high aloof
On pillars lofty, light and small;
The key-stone that locked each ribbed aisle,
Was a fleur-de-lys, or a quatre feuille;
The corbels were carved grotesque and grim,
And the pillars with clustered shafts so trim,
With base and with capital flourished around,
Seemed bundles of lances with garlands had bound.

There is no other remnant of antiquity in Scotland which has of late years been so much visited by strangers at Melrose. Since the publication of the poem in which the above lines occur the fame of the place has been carried wherever our language is known. This general admiration has caused a good deal to be done for the preservation of the ruin. In the market place stands an old cross. There is also a handsome episcopal church in the town. Near at hand is Old Melrose, the seat of W. Lockhart, Esq.

SELKIRKSHIRE
Which county returns one member.

GALASHIELS
A telegraph station. Hotels – Bridge Inn; Commercial; Victoria; Railway. Market Day – Tuesday. Fairs – Third Wednesday in March, July 8th, and October 10th.

A considerable trade in the manufacture of tartan and tweed cloths is here carried on. A fine church, three chapels, ten woollen mills, brewery, large tan yards, library, grammar school; close to which was the Hunting Tower of the Scottish Kings. Close at hand are Mugget Hill, Gala Water, Allan Water (the Glendeary of the Monastery), Lauder, Cowdenknowes, with its vitrified fort, and Ashestiel, where Scott wrote his Marmion.

Selkirk Branch
Galashiels to Selkirk

ABBOTSFORD
Telegraph station at Galashiels, 2½ miles. Hotel – The Abbotsford.

Abbotsford, 2 miles from Galashiels station, was the country seat of the great novelist and poet, Sir Walter Scott. This 'romance in stone' is an irregular, though picturesque, Gothic pile, begun by Scott in 1816, and completed as fancy or convenience dictated in the course of years. It overlooks the rippling Tweed, and the beautiful haughs of Ettrick on the opposite banks. The front is about 150 feet long. A fine entrance hall is ornamented with oak panelling, and blazoned coats of arms, by D. Hay. In the drawing-room is a collection of antique furniture, and portraits, among others, one of 'glorious John' Dryden – the 'great high priest of all the nine'. The armoury contains a great two-handed Swiss sword, the very counterpart of Rudolph Donnerhugel's, as described in Anne of Gierstein, and presented to Scott by his Swiss admirers; also King James's bottle, the great Marquis of Montrose's sword, Andrew Hofer's gun, Bonaparte's pistols, etc. Among the portraits in the dining-room are Cromwell, Graham of Claverhouse, Scott of Harden, and a curious one of Mary Queen of Scots' head on a charger. One room is full of drawings by Turner; another' is the library, 50 feet long, containing the Byron urn, the identical study where most of his delightful works were written, with his desk and clothes, which are preserved as memorials.

The visitor is also shown the various antiquarian relics, such as the pulpit of Erskine, the preacher, and the real iron-bound gate of the 'Heart of Mid-Lothian', or Edinburgh Tolbooth, which the mob attempted to burn in the Porteus riot. Scott died here in 1832, utterly broken down by the wonderful exertions he made to pay off the immense incumbrances in which his connection with the Ballantynes had involved him. As they brought him in, helpless with palsy, on his return from Italy, he murmured, 'Now I know I am at Abbotsford.' See Washington Irving's Abbotsford and Newstead Abbey, for an interesting account of his pilgrimage to this spot. It is an heirloom in the poet's family; but all his direct descendants are extinct.

From a hill near it about thirty places, celebrated in Scottish song, may be counted, a few of which are – Yarrow Braes, Ettrick Forest, Gala Water, the banks of Allan Water, the Bush aboon Traquair, Cowdenknowes, Melrose Abbey ruins, Selkirk, etc.

Lindean and Selkirk stations.

Peebles Branch
Eskbank to Peebles

On this branch the intermediate stations are Bonnyrigg, near which is an extensive colliery.

Hawthornden, close to which is the seat of Sir J. Drummond (the old residence of Drummond the poet, whom Ben Johnson came to see). It contains the dress which Charles Stuart wore in 1745, the Cypress Grove, celebrated by the poet, caves from which Ramsay of Bruce came out to assault the English, and was visited by Queen Victoria in 1848.

Roslin, at which are remains of a castle and chapel, beautifully situated in a fine glen, The grounds are turned into strawberry beds.

Penicuik, a large burgh, its population employed in weaving, and at the powder, paper, and saw mills. The church and house were built by Sir J. Clerk, Bart., both of which have noble porticoes; in the latter are a good library, fine

Peebles

Above: Peebles locomotive shed, 19 June 1936, with an ex-NBR 4-4-0 No. 9648 on shed. The driver and fireman stand in front of their locomotive. Peebles was the junction of both Caledonian and North British lines.

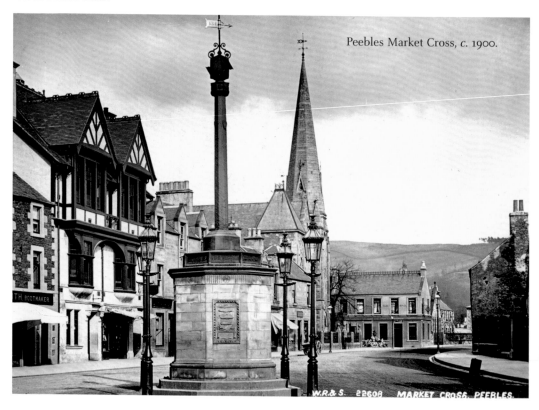

Peebles Market Cross, *c.* 1900.

gallery of paintings, Roman antiquities, Dundee's buff coat, which he wore at Killiecrankie, and in the grounds a pillar to Allan Ramsay, Arthur's Oven, Roman Temple, Fish Pond, Hurley's Cave, 150 feet long: and in the vicinity are the ruins of Ravensnook, the St Clair's seat, Brunstane, the Crichtons', etc.

Leadburn and Eddlestone, at which are the Druid's Hill, 2,100 foot high, traces of two camps, and the following seats: Cringletie, Lord Murray, and Portmore, w. Mackenzie, Esq.

PEEBLESSHIRE, or TWEEDDALE

When this county, which returns one member, is viewed from a distance, it appears to be one continued chain of hills, but on internal investigation, there are found along the sides of its rivers, many rich and fertile valleys of arable land. The county on the whole, however, is extremely mountainous, particularly along the southern side of the river Tweed. There is perhaps no river in Scotland on the banks of which there have been erected so many places for private defence against the hostile depredations of the borderers. Amid the many handsome country seats which now adorn its banks there are still to be seen the ruins of castles and towers, which exhibit the predatory spirit that prevailed formerly; yet, so great is the change, that there is probably no county in Scotland in which a more zealous and active spirit of agricultural improvement now prevails than in Peebles.

PEEBLES

A telegraph station. Hotel – Tontine. Market Day – Tuesday.
Fairs – 2nd Tuesday in Jan, and Oct, 1st Tuesday in March, 2nd Wednesday in May, Tuesday after July 18th, Tuesdays before August 24th, and Dec. 12th.

Peebles is an important Scottish burgh, and the capital of the county of that name, the inhabitants of which are mostly employed in the stocking and leather trade. Here James I composed 'Peblis to the Play', at Beltane Festival. The church, with a fine steeple, is built on the site of an old chapel and castle. Here is St Mungo's well, ruined chapels, camp at Cademuir Hill, Hill Forts, Dean's House, the seat of the late Lord March, and the scene of Scott's Maid of Neidpath, and Campbell's 'Earl March gazed on his dying child.' It is situated on the north bank of the Tweed, and is usually divided into the 'old' and 'new' towns. It is a place of great antiquity. The old town consists of little more than a single street, and has little of architectural uniformity to recommend it, but the new town is a very handsome suburb.

Above: By the 1950s, many of the branch lines had closed down. This view shows a ford that once went under the railway, which by the time of the image, had been closed, the track lifted and the bridge removed.

Above: Manse Bridge, Eddleston. Close to Eddleston is the 2,100ft Druid's Hill.

The Tweed, near Peebles.

Above: The countryside around Peebles, along the banks of the Tweed, is relatively prosperous agricultural land. Here, a man with two draught horses is harrowing a field.

Left: Kirkintilloch station staff in the 1920s, complete with station dog.

THE ARCHES, CASTLECARY.

Middle: Castlecary Arches on the main Edinburgh to Glasgow railway line. The station directly after the viaduct was the scene of a terrible accident on 10 December 1937, when two trains collided in a blizzard. Thirty-five died when an express ploughed into the rear of a stationary train.

Below: When this Bradshaw guide was written, the omnibus was horse-hauled. By the 1930s, the buses were motorised, and they served many outlying communities. Falkirk was home to Alexander's, who built buses close to the railway line at Camelon.

Intercity

Edinburgh and Glasgow
Glasgow to Edinburgh

On leaving Glasgow we are immediately plunged into a long tunnel, on emerging from which we soon reach BISHOP BRIGGS, and at a distance of 3¼ miles further, we arrive at CAMPSIE, the junction of the branch to Lennoxtown.

CAMPSIE BRANCH

Passing KIRKINTILLOCH and MILLTOWN stations we arrive at

LENNOXTOWN

Telegraph station at Glasgow, 11¾ miles.

Lennox Castle, the seat of J. Lennox, Esq., is in the vicinity.

Edinburgh and Glasgow Main Line continued

CROY – Near to this station are Holme, the seat of M. Rose, Esq. and Cantray, that of J. Davidson, Esq.
CASTLECARY – Here are the ruins of an ancient fort.
GREENHILL station.

FALKIRK

A telegraph station. Hotel – Red Lion.
Market Days – Thursday and Saturday.
Fairs – Last Thursday in January and October, (the largest in the country), first Thursday in March, April, and November, third Thursday in May and August, second Thursday in June and July.
Bankers – Clydesdale Banking Co.; Branch National Bank of Scotland; branch Bank of Scotland; branch of Commercial Bank of Scotland.
Money Order Office.

This town has a population of about 8,752, who return one member, and the county another one, and are employed in the iron, coal, leather and inland trade. It was occupied by the Pretender in 1745, who defeated General Hawley here, and the house at which he took up his quarters is still shown. The church, rebuilt in 1810 (in lieu of the old cruciform edifice built in 1105), contains tombs of Sir John the Græme, Stewart, who was killed in 1298, and the Monroes who fell in 1745. In the vicinity are Callander, seat of W. Forbes, Esq., M.P., Carron Hall, Col.

Canal near Nobel's Factory, Polmont.

Left: Before the railway, Glasgow and Edinburgh were connected by the Forth & Clyde and Union canals. Here, the Union Canal passes close to Linlithgow, at Polmont.

Middle: The Swedish chemist, Alfred Nobel, built an explosives factory in Linlithgow. Next to both canal and railway, it was a highly dangerous industy to locate in the middle of a small town. The next Nobel factory in Scotland was built at Ardeer in Ayrshire, in a more remote location.

Below: Slamannnan was a coal town, with numerous mines and pits in the vicinity. This view shows New Street, *c.* 1905.

NEW STREET, SLAMANNAN

Dundas. Bannockburn is near at hand. The proverb that applies to this place is, 'Ye're like the bairns of Falkirk, ye'll end ere ye mend.' In the vicinity of Almond inscriptions and urns have been found.

Passing POLMONT, the point of junction with the Scottish Central Railway, we very soon after enter the county of

LINLITHGOW

This county, which returns one member, does not possess that romantic scenery for which the Scottish mountains are so justly celebrated, but in many parts the estates are laid out with plantations formed in the very best taste, and in such a manner as to improve and shelter all the richer portions of the soil, and exhibit in its most beautiful aspects the face of the country. In the neighbourhood of Queensferry, by the sudden approximation of opposite promontories, the Forth is forced into a narrow strait, which on each side suddenly expands into an extensive bay, with richly ornamented banks. In every quarter, along the shores of the county, the Forth assumes a singular variety of aspects; hills, promontories, winding bays, lofty shores, and cultivated fields, bordering a fine sheet of water, a noble river, or a broad sea, according to the points of view in which it is seen.

LINLITHGOW

Telegraph station at Falkirk, 8 miles.

HOTEL – Star and Garter.

This town has a population of about 4,213 engaged in the cotton trade and the manufacture of leather. John, Earl of Stair, was a scholar at the Grammar School, where Kirkman was master. The church built by David L., and rebuilt in 1411, contains the tombs of the Livingstones and Dr Henry's Library and Catherine's Aisle, where James IV, it is stated, was forewarned of the Battle of Flodden Field. Close by it is the Palace on the Loch, of 80 acres, having fish and fowl. It was rebuilt by James IV, V, and VI, and contains some beautiful carvings in the Hall, Banquet Room, a Well, Parliament Hall, and Queen Mary's Room, from which there is a magnificent prospect. James V's jester (Rob Gib), was a native. The magistrates, trades, &c., ride the bounds in June.

Slamannan Branch

This branch turns off to the right, taking in the following stations: – BO'NESS, CAUSEWAYEND, BOWHOUSE, BLACKSTON, AVONBRIDGE (with a branch to BATHGATE, described below), SLAMANNAN, LONGRIGGEND, WHITERIGG, RAWYARDS, and AIRDRIE, at which place it unites with the Monkiand Railway.

51

Above: Winchburgh School, *c.* 1906.

Left: Upper Bathgate station.

Below: Rhoderic Dhu, an Improved Director-class locomotive on the Edinburgh-Glasgow route at Westercraigs on the line via Bathgate and Airdrie.

Edinburgh and Glasgow Main Line continued

WINCHBURGH – Here Edward II stopped after his defeat at the Battle of Bannockburn.

RATHO – Wilkie, author of 'Epigoniard,' was minister here. In the vicinity are Ratho Hall, seat of W. Hill, Esq.; Ratho House, R. Cadell, Esq.; Rathobyres, Danchead, Mrs Liston; Kaimes Hill, 680 feet high, and South Platt cairns, from which beautiful views may be obtained of the surrounding country.

Bathgate and Airdrie branch

This branch turns off to the right, and runs through BROXBURN, (near which is Broxmouth, the seat of the Duke of Buccleugh,) HOUSTON (where Cromwell routed Leslie), and LIVINGSTON, to

BATHGATE
A telegraph station.

Here a corn market is held on Wednesdays, and fairs on the first Wednesday after April, first Wednesday after the Term, fourth Wednesday in June and October, third Wednesday in July and August, Wednesday after Martinmas. The ruins of Walter Stewart's Castle, given to him by Bruce, may still be seen.

The stations next in succession are ARMADALE, WESTCRAIGS, FORRESTFIELD, CALDERCRUIX, CLARKSTON, and finally that of AIRDRIE, which forms a connecting link with the Caledonian and Monkland Railways.

Edinburgh and Glasgow Main Line continued

GOGAR – Here stone coffins have been found, and in the vicinity are Gogar House and Gogar Bank, two pretty seats.

CORSTORPHINE – This place is noted for its cream, and mineral spa. On the hill are several beautiful sents. The cruciform church was built in 1429, and contains effigies and arms of the Foresters, and Lantern to light travellers over the marsh, the expense of which is defrayed from the rent of Lamp Acre, in the possession of the master of the parish school. In the vicinity are Prestonfield, seat of Sir W. H. Dick, Bart., Belmont and Beechmont, two fine residences.

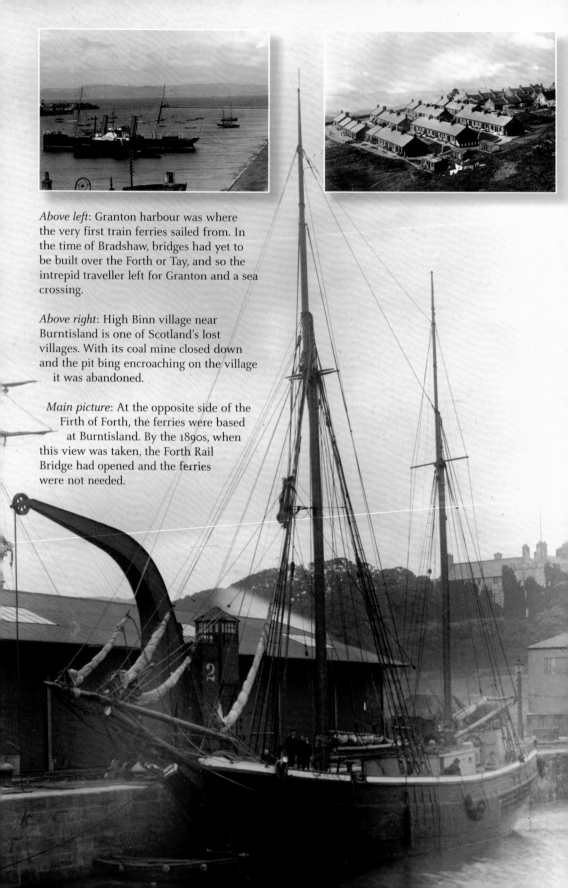

Above left: Granton harbour was where the very first train ferries sailed from. In the time of Bradshaw, bridges had yet to be built over the Forth or Tay, and so the intrepid traveller left for Granton and a sea crossing.

Above right: High Binn village near Burntisland is one of Scotland's lost villages. With its coal mine closed down and the pit bing encroaching on the village it was abandoned.

Main picture: At the opposite side of the Firth of Forth, the ferries were based at Burntisland. By the 1890s, when this view was taken, the Forth Rail Bridge had opened and the ferries were not needed.

Edinburgh via Fife to Dundee & Aberdeen

Edinburgh to Dundee and Perth

Leaving Princes Street, the railway runs on to Scotland Street, after which it divides into two branches, the one to the right running to the Docks at Leith; the other, via TRINITY station, to

GRANTON

    Telegraph station at Edinburgh, 3 miles.
    Hotel – Granton, Thomas Martin.
    Steamers – See Edinburgh
    Money order office at Edinburgh, 3 miles.

Here is an excellent pier, 1,700 feet, built by Walker, and a floating railway for luggage across to Burntisland, erected by Napier.

FIFESHIRE

Is an extensive maritime county in the eastern part of Scotland, and returns one member. The draining and cultivating of lands and lakes in all parts of this county has had a surprising and beneficial effect on the climate of the district. The fogs, which were constantly exhaling from the lochs and marshes, injured the crops of the better lands and afflicted the people with agues and other diseases. Fifeshire is divided into four districts: St Andrews, Cupar, Dunfermline, and Kirkcaldy. There are many ruins scattered over the surface of this county, consisting chiefly of castles and monastic establishments. The cattle of Fifeshire have long been in high repute, both as fattening and dairy stock.

BURNTISLAND

    A telegraph station. Hotel – Forth.
    Market Day – Saturday. Fair – July 10th.

This place has a population of about 2,724 engaged in the ship building, whaling, and coasting trade, and contains a pier harbour, used by the Romans, chapel, town house, market, distillery, bathing houses, schools, remains of the fortified walls and a fixed light on the pier. Here the General Assembly met in 1601. It was taken by Cromwell, and then by the Earl of Marr, in 1715. Rossend was built by the Druids. At Dunairn Camp there are fossils and volcanic remains.

Leaving KINGHORN we shortly arrive at ...

The Harbour, Kirkcaldy.

Above: The harbour at Kirkcaldy was all but abandoned by the 1930s. Here, a Coast Lines coaster is berthed. Kirkcaldy was famed for its Linoleum, the major manufacturer being Nairn's.

Middle: Cameron Bridge station.

Below: In the 1920s, an enterprising local used seashells and an old bus to make this decorative shell bus. For a time, it was a major tourist atraction in Leven.

SHELL BUS LEVEN

KIRKALDY, or KIRKCALDY

A telegraph station. Hotel – Railway.

Fairs – Third Fridays in February, July, and October.

Market Day – Saturday.

This town has a population of 10,470, who return one member, and are engaged in the linen trade. It contains six chapels, Town House, erected n 1830, Prison, Custom House, Gas and Water Works, Savings' Bank, Market House, Newsroom, Mechanics' Institution, factories, breweries, rope and linen factories, foundries distilleries. Grammar School, founded by Philip of Edenshead, who bequeathed £70,000 in 1828; Mason Lodge, Gilt Box Fund for seamen, a tidal harbour, but narrow, with a fixed light, which can be seen about nine miles distant; St Bryce's Church, with its old Norman portico; and Port Brae Church. Adam Smith was a native, in 1724. In the vicinity are Balwearel Tower, Ravenscraig Castle, Raith, seat of Colonel Ferguson, M.P. Dunniker, Lady Oswald.

Passing SINCLAIRTOWN, the next station we come to is

DYSART

Telegraph station at Thornton, 2¾ miles.

Hotel – Railway. Market Day – Saturday.

Fairs – May 6th, 3rd Tuesday in June, 4th Wednesday in August, and November 8th.

This place contains a population of about 8,041, who are employed in the weaving, ship building, and coasting trades, and has a Church, Chapel, Newsroom, Mechanics' Library, School, small tidal harbour, with a new dock, patent slip for repairs, and a forge, on the site of the Black Priory. Wallace, the mathematician, was a native in 1768. In the vicinity is Dysart House, seat of the Earl of Rosslyn.

THORNTON station, junction of the

Leven Branch

Passing CAMERON BRIDGE station, we arrive at

LEVEN

Telegraph station at Thornton, 5¾ miles.

Hotels – Crawford's; Star. Market Day – Saturday.

Fairs - 2nd Wednesday in April, 1st Wednesday in July, and 3rd Wednesday in October.

Here is a suspension bridge, which joins it to Dubbieside, a small harbour, library, two chapels, school, and flax factories.

From here the line continues through LUNDIN LINKS, and LARGO to

KILCONQUHAR, a small village situated in the midst of a hilly but fertile

Left: Cowdenbeath was a mining town, and there is no mistaking the traditional miners' rows. By the 1900s, many of these houses were slums and cleared soon after, with only a few surviving into the inter-war period.

Middle: Kinross Loch Leven locomotive shed on 17 June 1936. Just beyond is the railway station.

Below: Dunfermline is famed for weaving but it also has a historical abbey, where the remains of Robert the Bruce lie. However, in its vicinity is one of the world's most iconic structures, the Forth Rail Bridge, shown here with another British icon, Cunard's *Mauretania*, heading to Rosyth for scrap.

district, abounding in coal, limestone, &c. The project of extending the line to Anstruther, a seaport town in the district of St Andrews, and possessing direct communication with Edinburgh, has been entertained.

Dunfermline Branch
Thornton to Dunfermline

Passing the intermediate stations of CARDENDEN and LOCHGELLY we come to COWDENBEATH, the point of connection with the

Kinross-shire Railway

This short line of 7 miles re-opens a most interesting part of the country, closed, to a certain extent, for a length of time to the general traveller by the development of the railway system around having diverted the traffic from the great north road, which traversed this district.

From Cowdenbeath we pass en route the stations of KELTY and BLAIRADAM, arriving at the county town of

KINROSS

Market Day – Wednesday.
Fairs – March, 3rd Wednesday, o.s., June 12th, July, 3rd Wednesday, o.s., October 18th, o.s.

Situated on the west side of Loch Leven. It has a population of about 2,600, engaged in the weaving of linen and cotton.

Loch Leven is about 3½ by 2½ miles and 11 in circumference. It is studded with islands, on one of which – nearest to Kinross – stands the celebrated castle in which was imprisoned the ill-fated Queen Mary in 1567. It was here, too, she was compelled by Lord Lindsay to abdicate her claim to the Scottish crown; soon after which, by the aid of George Douglas, she escaped from the castle. The loch affords fine sport to the angler.

Dunfermline Branch continued

CROSSGATES and HALBEATH stations, at the latter of which there is good coal.

DUNFERMLINE

A telegraph station. Hotels – New Inn; Royal.
Market Day – Tuesday. Fairs – 3rd Tuesdays in January, March, April, June, July, September, October, and November.

This is a large burgh town, in the county of Fife, with a population of about 13,836, who are engaged in the diaper, damask, and fine linen manufactures, and

THE CROSS, FALKLAND.

Above: The steeple of the church at Markinch is 104 ft high.

Middle: The Cross at Falkland. The village was served by Falkland Road station, and a castle is located here. Famous residents have included Charles II and Rob Roy.

Below: Class J38 No 65901 passes Ladybank station on 26 April 1960 with an evening goods train.

contains three Churches, seven Chapels, Town House, in which is a shirt without seam, woven by Ingils; Guildry, with a spire 132 feet high; Mechanics' Institute School of Design, libraries, market, mills, breweries, gas works, soap, tobacco, and candle factories. Bridge over a glen, built by Chalmers of Pittenerief. St Leonard's Hospital. The church was rebuilt in 1820, and has a fine view over fourteen counties, from Ben Lomond to Loutra Hill; the nave of the old one still remains, in which lie buried Malcolm Canmore and his queen Margaret, whose shrine, in ruins, is shown. The bones of 'The Bruce' were reburied under the pulpit in 1818. There are ruins of the Abbey and part of the wall of the Abbey and part of the wall of the palace which James the First's queen built, where Charles I was born, and at which place he signed the covenant. Her bed is at Broomhall, and her cupboard at Pittencrief. It is built on an eminence, and has an irregular appearance, from its having been erected at various periods of time. The great object of attraction is its Abbey, part of which is now used as a Parish Church; the rest is in ruins, and convey but a faint picture of the former magnificence of the edifice.

Dunfermline has long been celebrated for different branches of weaving, but particularly that of table linen, which is said to be conducted more extensively here than in any other part of the United Kingdom. In the vicinity are Broomhall, seat of Lord Elgin; Pittencrief, J. Hunt, Esq.; Pitfirran, Sir J. Halket, Bart.; Leggie, Cavil, Pitbler, and Craiglascar Hill, with its Pictish Fort.

North British Main Line continued

MARKINCH

Telegraph station at Kirkaldy, 7¼ miles. Hotel – Galloway.

Fairs – Second Thursday in January, last Thursday in February, April, and June, first Thursday after August 12th, fourth Thursday in September, and Friday before Edinboro' Hallow Fair.

The church has a later steeple of 104 feet, stands on Markinch Hill, in which are some artificial terraces and the stob cross of stone 7 feet high. In the vicinity are Balgorice, Lord Levent; Balbirnie, J. Balfour, Esq.; Balfour, A. Bethune, Esq. (both old seats). A short branch, 4¾ miles, turns off here to the left to LESLIE, a village prettily situated on the river Leven, and noted for the stone coffins, &c., which have been discovered.

Passing FALKLAND ROAD, near to which is the town of Falkland, which contains a palace rebuilt by James V, who died here, on the site of Macduff's Castle, where the Duke of Albany starved his nephew Robert of Rothesay to death (see 'Fair Maid of Perth'), it has been a gate with a double tower, a large carved hall, and was occupied by Charles II, and Rob Roy in 1715. The forest in which James IV hunted no longer exists. There are camps at Dunshelt and Maiden Castle Hill.

We reach KINGSKETTLE, and then proceed on to LADYBANK, the junction of the ...

Above: Dollar was on the Devon Valley Line which trailed along the foot of the Ochils.

Left: Cupar station photographed in 1905.

Bottom left: Market Street, St Andrews, in the 1950s.

Fife and Kinross

This line branches off from Ladybank Junction, and communicates with the stations of AUCHTERMUCHTY, STRATHMIGLO, GATESIDE, MAWCARSE, MILNATHORT, HOPEFIELD, and finale with that of

Kinross, see page 59.

The Devon Valley lie commences at Hopefield and runs via CLEISH ROAD and CROOK OF DEVON to the Ochils, on the river Devon. There are waterfalls in the neighbourhood.

Dundee Branch
Ladybank to Leuchars

Passing SPRINGFIELD station, near which are Todd's large print works, we arrive at

CUPAR

Distance from station, ½ mile. A telegraph station.

Hotels – Tontine, Royal. Market Day – Thursday.

Fairs – 1st Thursday in January, May, June, July, August, and December,
3rd Thursday in February, 3rd Thursday and last Thursday in March, 2nd
Thursday in April and October, and November 11th.

This place has a population of about 5,686 employed in the coarse linen trade, and contains five chapels, town house, assembly rooms, academy erected on the site of the old castle, public library, gas works, almshouses, tanneries, tile, candle, and rope works, breweries, a collegiate church, rebuilt in 1785, retaining the steeple of the old one, which contains effigies of one of the Knights Templars. In the vicinity are Wemyss, seat of Capt. Wemyss, M.P., Carslogie Castle, R. Clephane, Esq., Pittencrieff, J. Huntley, The Mount, the old seat of Sir D. Lindsey, whose satires, &c., were acted at Playfield near the castle, and Garley Bank, where Argyle treated with the forces of the Queen Regent in 1559. Some cairns are also to be seen. The Scottish proverb for an obstinate man refers to this place: – 'He that will to Cupar maun to Cupar.'

Passing DAIRSIE we arrive at

LEUCHARS, near which are Leuchars House, seat of J. Lindsay, Esq., with ruins of an old castle, Pitlethie, the ancient hunting seat of James VI. Ardet, Pitcullo, and Drone, all fine noble seats. Leuchars is the junction of the

St Andrews Branch

GUARD BRIDGE station.

St Andrews

Above: St Andrews is full of buildings of antiquity. Being a religious settlement and an educational one for so long has left it with a rich heritage of architectural and historic gems. Here is St Rule's Tower in the 1890s. The tower itelf is some 180 ft high. The West Port is shown below, *c.* 1890.

ST ANDREWS

Telegraph station at Cupar, 12½ miles. Hotels – Cross Keys, Royal, Star. Market Day – Saturday. Fairs – 2nd Thursday in April, August 1st, and November 30th.

This old city is a parliamentary burgh with one member and university, and picturesquely seated on the cliffs, near the 'East Neuk' of Fife. The first view of its ruined towers and spires, the sea, and the cultivated environs, is very pleasing. Formerly it was the seat of an Archbishopric, an honour which it claimed from possessing the bones of St Andrew, the patron saint of Scotland. According to Fordun, St Rule or Regulus, who discovered these precious relics in 345, set sail from Patræ or Patras, in Greece, with the intention of carrying them to Constantinople, but, having no chart on board, was wrecked, after a long and painful voyage, in St Andrews Bay! A church was dedicated to this able navigator, and a large one was built over the prize he brought with him. This was the first foundation of the Cathedral, but the present structure dates only from the 12th century at the furthest. As usual it was a cross, 350 feet long, of which only the south walls and gable ends are left, the whole having been ruined at the Reformation by the adherents of John Knox, after a powerful sermon from him in 1559. Such had been the bitter persecution they sustained form the Romish party, and their infamous leader, Cardinal Beaton or Bethune, that they might be well pardoned for wishing to destroy every vestige of their power here.

Near this relic of antiquity is the very ancient tower of St Rule's Church, 180 feet high.

It is used as a sea mark, and a light is fixed to the cathedral for the same object at night. Close at hand are fragments of an Augustine priory, founded in 1120, and memorable as the place where Robert Bruce held his first parliament in 1309, when working out the independence of his country. The primate's seat or castle is here, overlooking the sea, from a window of which Boaton watched in triumph while his victim Wishart the martyr was dying at the stake; and here also, by a just retribution, this wicked oppressor was murdered by Norman Lesly in 1546. Patrick Hamilton and three others were also burtn by the dominant party. A bishop of Wishart's family founded a Dominican or black friary in the 13th century, of which there are still remains.

St Andrews is of so much historical celebrity, and so rich in memorials of the past, that no one can say he has seen Scotland who has not paid it a visit. Dr Johnson was here in 1773, in his tour with Boswell; in its streets, 'there is,' says he 'the silence and solitude of inactive indigence and gloomy depopulation' – a truly Johnsonian burst. Unfortunately it stands out of the beaten track. Something, however, has been done to redeem its neglected air, by a townsman, Major Andrews, who, while provost, exerted himself to stop the progress of decay, and introduced modern improvements. There are three principal streets, most of the houses of which are large and antique-looking; at the end of one, on the west side of the town, is an old gate, a remnant of the walls which surrounded it.

In the parish church is a fine monument to Archbishop Sharpe, 'that arch traitor to the Lord and his church,' as the Covenanters styled him, whom John Balfour of Burley, Hackstone of Rathillet, and others, barbarously murdered on Magus Muir. They were watching for another person when they met the unfortunate prelate. This muir is 3 miles from the city, and the exact spot where the bloody deed was perpetrated is marked by a stone in the midst of a fir wood, near the village of Boarhils. Its name properly is Mucross, from the boars which used to haunt it in such numbers that a boar is blazoned in the city arms.

Three colleges compose the University, which was founded in 1411, by Bishop Wardlaw. St Salvador (or Saviour's) is an unfinished quadrangle, 230 feet long, begun by Bishop Kennedy, whose effigies are in the chapel. St Leonard's was founded by Prior Hepburn in 1552; there is an old ruined Gothic church attached to it, and a modern one by the side. The third is St Mary's, which has been lately restored. About 150 students frequent this University. The library contains upwards of 50,000 volumes.

Close to the old priory of Blackfriars is another valuable institution, the Grammar School, which has been converted into The Madras College, at the instance of Dr Bell, a native, the author of the Bell (or monitor) system of teaching, which prevailed till lately in most of the national schools. He was chaplain to the East India Company, and left £60,000 to his native city for education. Here about 800 children are taught classics, mathematics, &c.

The harbour is rocky, and of little consequence. Formerly it had a good trade. One branch of manufacture still flourishes here, that of making balls for golf – a favourite game, played on the links or flat sands along the sea shore.

North British Main Line continued

Ladybank to Perth

From LADYBANK Junction we proceed to COLLESSIE station. In the vicinity near a mound are Maiden Castle, another camp, and Newtown, seat of C. Wallace, Esq.

NEWBURGH

Population about 2,638. Distance from station ¼ mile.
Telegraph station at Perth, 10¾ miles. Hotel – Mrs Anderson's.
Market Day – Saturday. Fairs – 3rd Friday in June and 1st Tuesday in September.

Ships of 500 tons burthen can come up to this place Salmon abounds, and in the vicinity are the ruins of an abbey, Mugdrum and Macduff crosses.

ABERNETHY

Telegraph station at Perth, 8½ miles.

Near ore, a round tower close to the church, 72 feet high, and 8 in diameter, in a good state of preservation. Pictish remains on Castle Law and Aberinthi, where King Malcolm met the conqueror in 1072.

BRIDGE OF EARN – This is a pretty watering place near Pitcaithley Spa, on the Earn river.

Dunfermline Branch
(Edinburgh and Glasgow)

Stirling to Dunfermline

Passing the station of CAUSEWAYHEAD, we next come to that of CAMBUS, which signifies the crooked turn of a river. A short railway turns off here, passing through MENSTRIE, to the town of ALVA, in a hilly district, at the foot of Bencleugh, the highest point of the Ochils.

ALLOA

A telegraph station. Hotels – Royal Oak, Crown.

Market Day – Wednesday and Saturday.

Fairs – 2nd Wednesday in February, May, August, and November.

This place, with a population of about 8,125, engaged in the shipping trade, collieries, corn, woolen, glass, tile and brick works, has two churches, one of which is pointed, with a steeple, and at which Fordyce was minister, five chapels, court house, custom house, assembly rooms, libraries, gas and water works, breweries, factories, and schools. The harbour has a good dry dock close to it. In the vicinity are Alloa House, the old seat of the Erskines, where James I was nursed; it has a tower of the thirteenth century, 30 feet high and 11 thick, and was partly burnt in 1800, and Shaw Park, Lord Mansfield.

A branch, 3¾ miles long, here diverges to the left for the accommodation of the town of TILLICOULTRY.

CLACKMANNAN

Telegraph station at Alloa, 2¼ miles.

Here is a school, at which M. Bruce the author of 'Lochleven' was master. In the vicinity are Clackmannan House, near which are Bruce's old tower and church, rebuilt in the pointed style by Gillespie, belonging to the Earl of Zetland, Kennetpans and Killaggie distilleries, Devon iron works, and Brucefield, the seat of Lord Abercrombie. The county returns one member jointly with Kinross-shire.

Left: Alloa's High Street in 1935. Alloa is still famous for its glass making and produces many millions of bottles a year. The town also once had its own harbour and even a shipbreaking yard. A railway crossed the Forth from South Alloa to the town, with a swing bridge to allow steamers heading for Stirling to pass.

Below: Dundee is famous for jam, jute and journalism. It was also home to one of Scotland's most famous photographers and postcard publishers; Valentine of Dundee. Here is a multiview postcard issued by the company to encourage sales of its postcards in the 1960s.

KINCARDINE

Telegraph station at Alloa, 3½ miles. Hotel – Union.

Market Days – Wednesday and Saturday.

Banks – Last Friday in July and Monday before Falkirk fair.

Here is a good pier and a cross 18½ feet high. The trade consists of shipbuilding, weaving, and sail making, which employ a population of about 2,697. This county returns one member.

Passing the stations of BOGSIDE and EASTGRANGE we soon reach Culross, at which there are remains of an abbey, founded in 1217, on the site of St ?'s Hermitage, by Malcolm of Fife, and since converted into a church, in which are effigies of the Bruces of Kinross. Close by are the ruins of the old church and St Mungo's chapel. Dunnemarle, with the ruins of the old castle where Lady Macduff and her sons were murdered by Macbeth; Gibscroft ? where Banquo in the 11th century fought the ?. Culross Abbey, seat of that brave old admiral the Earl of Dundonald, who first made coal tar here; it was built by Sir W. Bruce, and has since been rebuilt – and the salt pans and coal pits which went under the sea, and were visited by James VI, but which are not now worked. Its name signifies 'back peninsula.' Here at Tollzies are some Druid stones, and a companion of Lord Anson's built a house here called Tinian, after the Island at which the Centurion refitted in 1744.

Soon after passing the OAKLEY station we reach

Dunfermline, see page 59.

BROUGHTY (Ferry)

Population about 2,272. Telegraph station at Dundee, 4½ miles.

Hotel – Railway. Post Horses, Flys, etc., at the station and hotel.

Here are the ruins of an old castle, taken by the English after the battle of Prusey. It has a floating bridge to Ferry Port, and Claypotts Castle is close at hand.

Dundee, Perth, and Aberdeen

DUNDEE

A telegraph station. Hotels – Royal, British, Crown.

Market Days – Tuesday and Friday.

Fairs – Tuesday after July 11th, August 26th, and September 19th.

Bankers – British Linen Co.; Dundee Banking Co.; Bank of Scotland; National Bank of Scotland; East Bank of Scotland.

The capital of Forfarshire, seat of the Scottish linen trade, a port and burgh (returning one member), with a population of about 78,931, situated on the north side of the Tay. Coming direct from the metropolis, a ferry of two miles

Top: The pleasure steamer *Shamrock*, near Perth.

Left: Dundee Harbour with whalers drying sails.

Above: A Caledonian 4-4-0 steams past Magdalen Green.

must be crossed, from Broughty to Tay Port, in connexion with the railway. A swelling hill behind the town, called Dundee Law, is 525 feet high to the camp on the top. Here Montrose sat while his troops sacked the town, in 1645, after the battle of Tippermuir. Since 1815, Dundee has been greatly improved by the new quays, wet and graving docks, and the deepening of the chief harbour. About 50,000 tons of shipping belong to the port, a small portion being engaged in the whale fisheries. The factories for spinning and weaving flax exceed 100, employing as many as 16,000 hands, three-fourths of whom are women. Coarse linens, osnaburghs, diapers, sail-cloth, rope, canvas, &c., are the chief goods made up.

Near the harbour is the triumphal arch, 82 feet wide, built on the occasion of the Queen's visit in 1844. Among the modern improvements which have taken place in Dundee, may be noticed those in Union Street, which opens a communication with the Craig pier and the Nethergate; indeed, nearly all the old buildings have been superseded by new ones. In front of the quay, along the margin of the Tay, are the various docks and shipyards, terminated on the west by the Craig Pier, which is exclusively used for the large ferry steam-boats. On the east the piers project into the deep water, on which are placed various coloured lights to guide the seamen after sunset. Opposite the town is a beacon, which is built on a dangerous rock. Nearly the whole of the space now appropriated to the docks, was originally a semicircular sandy beach, but by great exertion the spirit inhabitants have erected a series of quays which are unequalled in Scotland. There are 20 churches and chapels. Three churches stand together on the site of that founded by William the Lion's brother, David (there here of Scott's 'Talisman') in pursuance of a vow made at sea on returning from the Crusades; its square tower, 156 feet high, still remains, though damaged by a fierce storm in 1840. David also built a castle, which figures in the war of independence as having been taken by Wallace and Bruce. The former great patriot was educated at the priory in this town, and made himself known, about 1271, by killing Delly, an insolent young Norman knights in the Governor's train. The Town House in High Street, was built by Adams, in 1734; other buildings are, the Exchange, Trades Hall, Academy, St. Andrew's Church, with a tall spire, &c.

Some of the oldest houses are in Seagate. High Street and Murraygate are the most bustling thoroughfares. When Charles II was crowned at Scone in 1650, by the Covenanters, he came to reside at Whitehall, in the Nethergate, since pulled down. Another house, in the middle of High Street, was occupied by Monk (after taking the town by storm in 1645); and by the Pretender, in 1716; it was also the birthplace of Moumouth's widow, Anne, Duchess of Buccleugh (the Lady of Brankxholme Tower, in the 'Lay of the Last Minstre.' In the Cowgate is an arch from which Wishart, the martyr, preached during the plague of 1544, the infected part of his congregation being kept by themselves on one side. Towards Dundee Law, at the end of Dunhope Wynd, is Dunhope Castle (now a barrack), which belonged to the Scrymgeours, (hereditary standard-bearers of Scotland), and to the famous Graham of Claverhouse, whom James II create Viscount Dundee, before his death at Killiecrankie. Mackenzie, the great lawyer, and Ivory, one of the first mathematicians of modern days, were natives of Dundee, a name supposed to be derived from Donum-Dei or, God-given, applied to it by David, its founder.

Within a short distance are, Broughty Castle; Gray the seat of Lord Gray; Camperdown, that of Lord Duncan; and Mains, another of Claverhouse's seats.

Passing BROUGHTY FERRY and MONTFIETH (which has an old castle, and in the vicinity The Grange, an old seat, and Fintry), BARRY (near which is an oval camp 168 yards round, where it is reported that King Arthur's wife Vanora was confined by the Piets), CARNOUSTIE, and EAST HAVEN stations, we arrive at

ARBROATH

Population about 10,030. A telegraph station.
Hotels – Albion, White Hart, Royal. Market Day – Saturday.
Fairs – January 31st, 3rd Wednesday in June, and July 18th.
Bankers – Branch of British Linen Co.; Branch of Commercial Bank of Scotland.

WEST COAST CORRIDOR EXPRESS AT DUNDEE.

A Caledonian Cardean-class 4-6-0 at Dundee on the express to Aberdeen via Forfar.

A port and parliamentary burgh, in Forfar. Its proper name is Aberbrothock, signifying that it is situated at the mouth of the Brothock, which here falls into the North Sea. Provisions, paving-stone, linen (which is the staple manufacture and bone-dust, are its chief exports; and about 8,000 tons of shipping are registered as belonging to the port. Formerly it was noted for a rich mitred abbey, founded in 1178, by King William the Lion, who was buried in it. All that remains of this gorgeous pile is the ruined church, 270 feet long, with its cloisters and fine east window. The latter has a circular light at the top, forming a conspicuous mark for seamen coming into harbour, who call it the 'Round O of Arbroath.' The three rows of blind arches on the wall produce a fine effect. The chapter house, great gate, and prison, are also left. The portcullis of the abbey figures in the town arms. Close to the site is a modern Parish Church, with a spire 150 feet high. A signal tower here communicates with the famous bell Rock Lighthouse, which is 10 miles south-east out at sea, opposite the mouth of the Tay, and is the Inch-Cape Rock of Southey's well-known lines – a dangerous reef of red sandstone, 2,000 feet long, which was under the special care of the abbots: –

> With neither sign nor sound of shock
> The waves flowed over the Inch-Cape Rock.
> So little they rose, so little they fell,
> They did not move the Inch-Cape bell.
> The pious Abbot of Aberbrothock
> Had placed that bell on the Inch-Cape Rock:
> On the waves of the storm it floated and swung,
> And louder, and louder, its warning rung.
> When the rock was hid by the tempest's swell
> The mariners heard the warning bell
> And then they knew the perilous rock.
> And blessed the Abbot of Aberbrothock.

There is a bell swung in a wicker frame, something like this, at the corner of a bank at the entrance of Southampton Water, called Jack-in-the-Basket. As to the Inch-Cape bell, the story is, that it was wantonly cut adrift by a pirate, to plague the Abbot, and that his vessel was soon after wrecked on the very rock. In 1807-11, a noble lighthouse was built by Stevenson, on the model of Smeaton's at the Eddystone, which is shaped like the trunk of a tree. It is of solid stone for 30 feet upwards, the total height being 115 feet. The stone blocks are dove-tailed together; there are five stories above. At the base the diameter is 42 feet, which lessens to 15 feet at the top. The light itself is alternately bright and red every two minutes, and can be seen 14 miles off. In foggy weather a bell is tolled. Four men live here, each of whom every six weeks, for a change, takes a fortnight's turn ashore, and there is no want of candidates for this office.

Lighthouses of equal beauty and solidity have been built on this plan upon the Black Rock at Liverpool, and Skerryvore, in the Western Islands.

Above: Arbroath is famous for Kerr's Miniature Steam Railway, which runs alongside the main line to Aberdeen. The company also operated these miniature buses in the early 1960s.

Above: Dundee was at one point a major locomotive manufacturing city. Carmichael's built this engine in 1833. for the Dundee & Newtyle Railway. It was withdrawn in 1854.

Left: On Christmas Day 1950, the Stone of Destiny was stolen from Westminster Abbey. It was eventually recovered in Arbroath Abbey, after months of searching by the police.

Passing COLLISTON, LEYSMILL and FRIOCKHEIM, we reach GUTHRIE, where is a Roman camp, and in the vicinity Guthrie House, seat of J. Guthrie, Esq., with an old tower 60 feet high and 10 thick, erected by Sir Alexander Guthrie, who was slain at Flodden Field. The church was built by Lord Treasurer Guthrie.

Scottish North Eastern

Perth to Forfar and Aberdeen

Passing LUNCARTY (near which is the largest bleaching field in Scotland, on which Kenneth III, with the aid of the Hays, routed the Danish Pirates in 972), we arrive at

STANLEY (Junction)
A telegraph station.

Here a small spinning trade is carried on by the inhabitants. Population, about 1,980.

Stanley to Cupar

Passing BALLATHIE we reach CARGILL station, near which is Shortwood Shaw, Wallace's hiding place. Close by are ruins of a cell, Druidical circles, tumuli, Castiehill Roman camp and road, Stoball, an old seat of the Drummond's, where Annabella, wife of Robert III, and ancestress of the Stuarts, was born. Pearl mussels have been found here.

WOODSIDE station.

COUPAR ANGUS, or CUPAR
A telegraph station.
HOTEL – Strathmore Arms.
MARKET DAY – Thursday.
FAIRS – Tuesday before Old Christmas, 3rd Thursday in March, May 26th, 1st Tuesday in October, and Thursday on or after November 22nd.

This place has a population of about 2,004 engaged in the bleach-fields, tanneries, distilleries, and linen factories. It contains three chapels, town hall, schools, public library, meal mills, traces of an old abbey, in which was found an almanae with Arabic figures, dated 1432, and a church, close to which some stone coffins have been discovered.

Blairgowrie Branch
ROSEMOUNT station.

BLAIRGOWRIE

POPULATION, about 3,014. A telegraph station.

HOTEL – Robertson's. MARKET DAY – Saturday.

FAIRS – 3rd Wednesday in March, May 26th, 2nd Wednesday in August, 1st Wednesday in October and November.

This place is situated on the river Ericht, which abounds with fish. It is celebrated for its pure white marble, highly esteemed by sculptors and architects. In the vicinity are Craighall Ratray, from which some fine views may be obtained, Ardblair, and Newton House, the seat of the McPhersons.

Scottish North Eastern Main Line continued

ARDLER station.

MEIGLE

A telegraph station.

Junction with Newtyle and Dundee; it is also the point of deviation of a short line, via FULLARTON and JORDANSTOWN, to ALYTH. In the churchyard at Meigle are some antique sculptured stones to Vanora the wife of King Arthur, who was taken away by his nephew Mordred, and concealed at Buryhill Camp, which is partly vitrified, and 180 feet high by 72. The Belliduff Tumulus has a granite pillar; and in the vicinity are Belmont, the seat of Lord Wharncliffe; Kinloch, J. Kinloch, Esq.; and Drumkilbo. A market is held here on Wednesdays, and there are fairs on the last Wednesday in June and October.

Forfarshire, or Angus

This county, which returns one member, includes the districts of Glenisla, Glenesk, and Glenpressin. Its scenery is extremely beautiful, and presents a variety of picturesque views, not excelled by any other Scottish county. The great level valley of Strathmore runs through the centre of Forfarshire from east to west; and the lines of hills which border this extensive tract of country, with the Grampians on the north, and some minor ranges on the south, may be said to form the county into a series of continuous ridges, generally pursuing a direction from east to west. The portion of the Grampians in this county contains many fine vallies.

DUNDEE AND NEWTYLE

NEWTYLE

POPULATION, about 1,141.

HOTEL – Strathchurch.

In the vicinity are Hatton Castle in ruins, which was built in 1575, by Lord Oliphant; castle of Balcraid and Auchtertyre Camp, both ruins; at the latter of which Montrose rested. From Kilfarnie Beacon a view of ten counties is obtained, as far as St Abb's Head, on a clear day.

Passing HATTON, near which is the fine seat of General Arbuthnott, M.P., we soon reach AUCHTERHOUSE, the castle near which is the seat of Lady H. Wedderburn, and then proceed to DRONLY, thence to BALDRAGON (near which is the handsome seat of Sir J. Ogilvie, Bart.), LOCHEE, CAMPERDOWN, and LIFF, arrive at

Dundee, see page 69.

Scottish North Eastern Main Line continued

Meagle to Kirriemuir Junction

Passing EASSIE, close to which are Dunkenny, the seat of J. L'Amy, Esq., and Nevay, the Right Hon. Stewart Mackenzie, we proceed to GLAMMISS, where there is a fair held in June, and near which is the Castle in which Malcolm II was murdered in 1033. It was given to J. Lyon by his father-in-law, Robert II in 1372, and contains some of the old turrets, walls 15 feet thick, suits of armour, 150 portraits, and some antique sun dials, &c.; close to the Manse is a pillar to King Malcolm, also one at Cossans, and an old fort at Dunoon, all worth a visit. Soon afterwards we reach the station at

KIRRIEMUIR (Branch)

POPULATION about 7,617. A telegraph station.

HOTEL – Commercial. MARKET DAY – Friday.

FAIRS – March 13th, Friday after May 26th, 1st Wednesday in June and November, July 24th, and Wednesday after November 18th.

BANKERS – National Bank of Scotland, G. Brand, Esq., Manager; draw on Glyn and Co.

Scottish North Eastern Main Line continued

FORFAR

A telegraph station.

HOTELS – County Arms, Morrison's.

MARKET DAYS – Wednesday and Saturday.

FAIRS – Last Wednesday in February, Second do in April, 1st do. in May, 1st Tuesday and Wednesday in July and August, last Wednesday in September, 2nd do. in October, and 1st do. in November.

BANKERS – Branch of Bank of Scotland; Branch of British Linen Co; Branch of Commercial Bank of Scotland; Branch of National Bank of Scotland; North of Scotland.

Left: Hand loom weaving was once a major industry in Forfar, but by the late 1890s, when this photograph was taken, it was in decline.

Middle: The North Lodge of Glamis Castle.

Below: This bridge over the North Esk was rather damaged when it collapsed as a traction engine drove through the parapet. The crowd of onlookers views the remains of the traction engine.

The town of Forfar, with a population of about 9,311, engaged in the shoe and weaving trades, is situated in the romantic valley of Strathmore, and is of considerable antiquity. It has lately received many additions to its general appearance. Amongst those edifices which form the most prominent features in the modern improvements are a handsome range of county buildings in Castle Street, an Episcopal chapel, excellent subscription room, library, town house, which contains the bridle with which people were harnessed previous to being burnt at 'Witches' Howe'; news room, school, academy, and a church lately rebuilt, which has an old bell, the gift of Strange, a native. The Loch should be visited, as it contains the ruins of Queen Margaret's Nunnery. In the vicinity are Restenet Priory, and Finhaven Castle, at which the Earl of Crawford received James II. Don the botanist was born here in 1800.

Passing CLOCKSBRIGGS we soon reach AULDBAR ROAD station, close to which is the fine seat of P. Chalmers, Esq.

GUTHRIE (Arbroath Junction)

Telegraph station at Forfar, 7 miles.
MONEY ORDER OFFICE at Brechin, 5 miles.

Here are a Roman Camp not far from the station, and Guthrie House, seat of J. Guthrie, Esq.

Passing FARNELL ROAD, close to which are the ruins of Airley Castle, and Kinnaird, the seat of the Carnegies (in the vicinity fine trout and salmon may be caught), we proceed to the

BRIDGE OF DUN (which signifies Fort), near which is the fine seat of the Marchioness of Ailss, Dun House, and the salmon fisheries.

BRECHIN (Branch).

A telegraph station. HOTEL – Commercial.
MARKET DAY – Tuesday. FAIRS – 3rd Tuesday in January, 3rd Wednesday in April, 2nd Wednesday in June and two following days, July 2nd, Monday before last Wednesday in September. BANKERS – Branch of British Linen Co.

This town has a population of about 6,637 employed in the making of osnaburghs, sail-cloth, and brown linen; and contains five chapels, town house, academy (the master is also a preceptor of Maison Dieu founded by Wm. de Brochin, in 1205), mechanics' institute, hospital, dispensary, brewery, distilleries, spinning mills, and a Collegiate Church, built in 1808 near the spire of St Ninian's Cathedral, at which there is a leaning round tower, 108 feet high, and at Abernathy is a similar one. In 1572 the battle of Brechin was fought, between James II and the Crawfords, when the Marquis of Huntly defeated the latter. The Danes burnt the town in 1012, and Montrose destroyed it in 1645. It is the bishop's seat, and near at hand is Panmure Castle, the seat of Lord Panmure, which is built on the site of the old one taken by Edward I in 1303.

Montrose
The harbour in the early 1900s.
From fishing boats to small-scale
shipbuilding, the harbour is now home
to oil rig support vessels. A shipyard
in the town even built a famous
Cunarder, the *Alsatia*, used as a
tender at Cherbourg.

DUBTON Junction

Telegraph station at Montrose, 3 miles.
MONEY ORDER OFFICE at Montrose, 3 miles.

MONTROSE (Branch)

A telegraph station. HOTELS – Star, White Horse, Albion.
MARKET DAY – Friday. FAIRS – Friday after Whitsuntide and Martinmas.
BANKERS – Branch of Bank of Scotland; Branch of British Linen Co.; Branch of
National Bank of Scotland; Branch of East Bank of Scotland.

MONTROSE, in Forfarshire, was called Munross, as it stands on a little headland
(ross in Gaelic*, rhos in Welsh) between the north sea and its harbour, which
is a natural lake or basin, a little up the South Esk, inside the town. This basin,
though 3 miles in circuit, is very shallow; wet docks have been constructed, and
about 15,000 tons of shipping belong to the port. Over a part of the river is one
of Sir S. Brown's suspension bridges, built in 1829, 432 feet long, and lying on
towers 72 feet high.

*another derivation makes it Mons Rosarum, or Mount of Roses; and, accordingly,
on the town seal is a wreath of roses, with a motto signifying that the sea enriches
and the Rose embellishes.*

As a parliamentary burgh, Montrose returns one member, and has a population
of about 15,238, many of whom are engaged in the linen manufacture. The late
member, the estimable and patriotic Joseph Hume, Esq., was a native of this place,
from which he was sent to India, under the patronage of the Panmure family,
where he did great service as a Persian scholar. Another native was the late Sir
Alexander Burnes, a kinsman of the poet Burns, who was assassinated at Cabool
in 1841, on the outbreak of the Afghan war. The great Marquis of Montrose was
also born here in 1612, in the hosue afterwards occupied by the Chevalier on his
landing in 1716. Another local event is that related by Froissart of the Douglas,
the 'good Lord James,' who, in 1330, embarked here with the heart of Bruce for
the Holy Land. He was killed before he got there, having landed at Seville to fight
the Moors; while the casket containing the King's heart was brought home and
buried at Melrose.

The site of the town is flat, but there are some moderate hills (Three Horns,
&c.), in the environs, from which is a goodly prospect of the town, basin, and the
distant Grampians. When the rtde is up the basic appearance is like an animated
lake, at the bottom of a cultivated amphitheatre, green to the water's edge, and
covered with gardens and country houses.

The basin above alluded to is nearly dry at low water, but is so completely
filled up by every tide as to wash the garden walls on the west side of the
town, and to afford sufficient depth of water in the channel for allowing
small vessels to be navigated three miles above the harbour. At high water,

Above: Montrose engine shed on 8 June 1936, with 4-4-0 no. 9136 next to the water tower. Montrose's famous steeple can be seen in the background.

Below: Kincardineshire is a predominantly agricultural county. Cissy Wood, shown near Stonehaven, is ploughing in a way that Bradshaw would have recognised. Would he recognise the tractors and highly specialised farming equipment of today?

the appearance of Montrose, when first discovered from the public road on the south, is peculiarly striking, and seldom fails to arrest the eye of the stranger. The basin opening towards the left, in all the beauty of a circular lake; the fertile and finely cultivated fields rising gently from its banks; the numerous surrounding country seats which burst at once upon the view; the town, harbour, and bay stretching further on the right; and the lofty summit of the Grampians, nearly in the centre of the landscape, closing the view towards the north-west, altogether present to the eye of the traveller one of the most magnificent and diversified amphitheatres to be found in the United Kingdom. The South Esk is crossed by a magnificent suspension bridge, which stretches aross the river in a noble span, the distance between the points of suspension being 432 feet. The town consists chiefly of one spacious main street, from which numerous lanes run off on each side, as from the High-street of Edinburgh.

None of the buildings are of much account. The Town Hall and Linen Hall are in High Street. The Academy may be known by its dome, and the Parish Church by the spire: the Public Library is of old date. The favourite game of golf is played on the sandy links along the shore; and here (where the races are held) the Queen's Scottish Body Guard of Archers met in 1850 to compete for prizes. Fish, viz., salmon, lobsters, cod, &c., are abundant, the cod being caught at Montrose Pits, in the North Sea – a singular hollow, which is 30 fathoms deeper than the tract around.

All this part of the line passes through the fertile Vale of Strathmore.

Scottish North Eastern Main Line continued

Dubton to Aberdeen
CRAIGO station, near which is Craigo House, the seat of T. Carnegie, Esq.

KINCARDINESHIRE
Is now almost exclusively of an agricultural character, for though it has a sea-coast of considerable extent, it possesses no harbour of any eminence. The soil is of a very productive kind, and is cultivated in a style nowhere surpassed in Scotland. The county, in its more level parts, is highly embellished with the country seats of its numerous resident proprietors, each amid its own thriving woodland. This county returns one member.

MARYKIRK
Telegraph station at Laurencekirk, 3¼ miles.

At the old church here are tombs of the Strachans, Thorntons, Barclays of Balmachewan, stone cross and antique font. In the vicinity are Balmachewan, seat of Col. Fraser; Inglismaldie, Earl of Kintore; Halton Castle, General Arbuthnott,

Aberdeen

Above: Charabancs await passengers at Castle Street, Aberdeen, in the 1930s. Despite being an industrial city, Aberdeen was also a tourist centre, with its fine beaches and spectacular views.

Above: The steamer *Crankland* is berthed outside the Harbour Bar, with her crew no doubt inside while railwaymen unload a steamer of coal into waiting GNSR wagons.

Bottom: Aberdeen's fishing industry was huge but has now been replaced by oil, making Aberdeen one of Britain's boom cities.

Aberdeen Fishing Industry.
Cleaning Haddocks.

M.P.; Kirktonhill, R. Taylor, Esq.; the Druid's Stones at Hospital, Balankillie, &c.; and Inglisburn at which a battle was fought with the English.

LAURENCEKIRK
A telegraph station.

Celebrated for the manufacture of wooden snuff boxes. Here Dr Pitcairn found Ruddiman, the Latin grammar author, master of the school. Beattie, the poet, and opponent of Hume, in his Essay on Truth, was a native. Fairs – 3rd Wednesday in January, last Tuesday in April, 26th May, Thursday after 3rd Tuesday in July, November 22nd, Thursday after 2nd Tuesday in August, Monday before last Wednesday in September, 1st Thursday in November. Markets on Monday.

FORDOUN
(Telegraph station at Laurencekirk, 3¼ miles.)

Near which Montrose took up his position on the eve of the battle at Kilsyth. The church, which was rebuilt, is near Luther Water, a pretty spot; here are two Roman camps, 249 feet, and a British one close to Drumsleid. The mineral springs are considered good. The learned and eccentric lawyer, Lord Monbodde, was a native. Fordoun, the author of the Scotichronicon, was a monk here; and Beattie kept a school until his advancement. Three miles beyond is the now insignificant village of Kincardine, which was the capital of that county until James VI's time, where are the ruins of Kenneth III's Castle, who was killed at Fettercairn.

We then proceed to DRUMLITHIE station, after which we arrive at

STONEHAVEN
Distance from station, 1½ mile. A telegraph station.
MARKET DAY – Thursday. FAIRS – Thursday before Candlemans, day before May 26th, 3rd Tuesday in June, 2nd Tuesday in August, 2nd Tuesday in October, day before Nov. 22nd, Thursday before Christmas day.
BANKERS – Bank of Scotland; Aberdeen Town and County, and North of Scotland.

Since the reign of James VI this place has been the county town of Kincardineshire, and contains a population of about 3,240, who are principally engaged in the herring fisheries, distilleries, and breweries. It has a market house, town hall, dispensary, bridge over the Cowie which joins the old and new towns, water and gas works, quay, Donaldson's free school, a pier, with two fixed lights, which can be seen at a distance of 13 miles; a harbour, with 16 feet of water; two good churches, and four chapels.

Passing MUCHALLS, NEWTON HILL, PORTLETHEN, and COVE stations, we enter ...

ABERDEENSHIRE

Which is one of the most extensive counties in Scotland, and returns one member. It forms the north-east corner of the island, being the eastern-most point of a large triangle, which juts out far into the German Ocean, and is circumscribed by lines running between Edinburgh, Inverness, and Peterhead. The greater part of it may be denominated a level plain, agreeably diversified by irregular depressions, and gently swelling slopes, forming a congeries on pleasing knolls, with vales between, each intersected by its little rill, so as to exhibit the scenery, the general appearance of which is tolerably uniform, though its particular features are varied at every step.

ABERDEEN

POPULATION about 71,973. Telegraph station at the railway station.

HOTELS – Douglas, near the station; Royal; Aberdeen.

MARKET DAYS – Thursday and Friday.

FAIRS – First Wednesday in April, last Wednesday in August, 2nd Friday in May and November, 1st Tuesday in every month at Bridge of Don; last Thursday in April and 1st Wednesday in November at Old Aberdeen; also every Wednesday, for cattle, in King Street.

BANKERS – Aberdeen (incorporated with the Union), Town and County, and North of Scotland.

ABERDEEN (OLD) is a place of great antiquity. It lies about a mile to the north of the new town, near the mouth of the river Don, over which there is a fine single-arched Gothic bridge, which rests on a rock on each side, and is universally admired. This town consists chiefly of one long street.

ABERDEEN (NEW), the capital of the county, is considered the third city of importance in Scotland. It lies on a slightly elevated ground on the north bank of the river Dee, near its efflux into the sea, and about a mile and a half from the mouth of the Don. It is a large and handsome city, having many spacious streets, lined on each side by elegant houses, built of granite from the neighbouring quarries.

Aberdeen derives its name from the Dee, on the north bank of which it lies, not far from the Devana of Ptolemy, and the river's mouth ('aber' in Gaelic), which makes an excellent port, whence cotton, linen, woollen goods, combs, and writing papers in large quantities, granite, cattle, and agricultural produce from the interior, salmon, &c., are exported in great quantities. The salmon is sent to Billingsgate Market packed in ice, an ingenious plan for preserving it, which was first adopted here. The fisheries on the Dee, worth £10,000 a year to the city, were originally granted by Bruce, on account of the gallant behaviour of the people in driving out the English garrison planted here by Edward I. their watchword was 'Bon Accord,' which is the motto of Aberdeen to this day. A history of the town has been written under this title. Its harbour, improved by Telford at a great cost, contains 34 acres, the pier is 1,200 feet long. Recently a large wet dock has been constructed, for the shipping of which there are registered at the port 230, nearly 70,000 tonnage.

Most of the houses are built of white granite, which gives it a handsome and durable appearance. The almost inexhaustible supplies of this stone are close at hand. Leaving the old 'Brig o' Dee,' or Dee Bridge, above the suspension bridge, where Montrose, in one of his descendents, fought a battle with the Covenanters and walking about a mile, we find ourselves in a fine street of high stone houses, called Union Street, a mile long, which leads over the Denburn (a raving crossed by a dry bridge) to Castle Square, in the centre of the town, where it meets Castle Street, in a square surrounded by high houses. The principal buildings stand in these two thoroughfares. Near the site of the old castle, which Edward I besieged in 1298, is an octagonal building (the market cross), in the Gothic style, with medallion heads of Scottish Kings, and coasts of arms upon it, first built in 1686, and restored in 1842. Close to this is a statue of the Duke of Gordon, a branch of which family (Earl of Aberdeen), lately Prime Minister, takes his title from this city.

Not far off, a spire, 120 feet high, marks the Town House, built in 1730; it has portraits by Jameson, a native of Aberdeen, with an armoury. The new Assize Court and Prison stand on the site of the old Tolbooth, or 'Mids o'Mar,' i.e., Middle of Mar, as the district round Aberdeen is called. The Earl of Mar, it will be remembered, was one of the most devoted partisans of the Stuarts; but the citizens, as a commercial body, were too 'Aberdeen awa',' as they say, to mix themselves up with his projects. Some of the handsomest buildings in this city are the County Rooms in Union Street (with portraits by Lawrence and Pickersgill), Athenæum News Room, and Aberdeen and North of Scotland Banks, mostly in the Grecian style, for which the granite is best suited. Some idea of the prosperity and importance of Aberdeen may be derived from the fact that the deposits in the local banks amount to three millions sterling. The new markets are 315 feet long.

The East and West churches, though in the Gothic style, are both modern, and close to the site of St Nicholas's old church, the tower of which is see in the East Church. Beattie, the poet of the 'Minstrel,' is buried in the latter. The North Church has a fine spire of 159 feet. Altogether there are between 20 and 30 churches and chapels, including four for the Episcopalians.

There are many educational and benevolent establishments, among which, the Grammar School (built in 1757, but founded as far back as 1418), Dr Bell's Schools, Gordon of Straloch's Hospital (lately enlarged), Deaf and Dumb School, the Infirmary, &c., may be noticed. Barbour Jameson, Gregory, Abercrombie, Gibbs, Anderson, Bishop Elphinstone, Dunbar, Patrick Forbes, Burnet, T. Reid, and R. Hamilton, were natives. One of the first printed Scottish books was the 'Breviary of Aberdeen.' In Broad Street Byron lived in his youth. His mother was a Gordon.

MARISCHAL COLLEGE, founded in 1393 by the Keiths, Earls Marischal (or Marshal) of Scotland, but rebuilt of granite, in the Gothic style, by Simpson, in

Above: One of Aberdeen's major industries was quarrying of granite. Here, a quarry at Kemnay is being worked in the 1920s.

Below: Kittybrewster locomotive sheds in the 1920s.

1837. It is an imposing pile, with a tower 100 feet high; the museum is 74 feet long, and contains portraits by Jameson, the 'Scottish Vandyck,' who was an excellent painter. His daughter, too, was an artist; some of her embroidery used to adorn St Nicholas's Church. Above 20 professors are attached to this college, which numbers 600 students designed chiefly for the church and parochial schools. One of the Gregorys connected with this university invented the reflecting telescope.

At OLD ABERDEEN is King's College, with 360 students, founded in 1494; like its fellow it is in the Gothic style, and has a very elegant tower, a lantern on springers, an ancient chapel, and a library of 35,000 vols., with portraits by Jameson; Hector Boece, the first principal, is buried in it. Here also is the old Cathedral, the seat of a bishop in Episcopal times; it contains many tombs, blazoned arms in the oak ceiling, and a beautiful west window. This old part of the town is on the Don, which falls into the sea about half a mile beyond Balgownie Bridge, a curious Gothic arch, 67 feet span, built by Bruce between two dark rocks. Byron refers to it, and the legend connected with it, in Don Juan. There is a new bridge, remarkable from the fact that it was built from a bequest of £2 5s in the time of James VI, which, with care and economy, amounted to £20,000 a remarkable instance of how money accumulates at compound interest.

Besides cotton and woollen mills, ironworks, and ship-yards, Aberdeen possesses granite polishing works, all of which deserve notice. Its fine steamers and clippers, with the 'Aberdeen bow,' are well known.

Above: Having just departed from Aberdeen, the 1.10 p.m. down service to Edinburgh via Arbroath passes workmen's camps in the fields in the 1930s.

Above: By the early 1900s, the Great North of Scotland Railway was using buses to extend rural services, such as here at Methlick.

Middle: Banchory station in 1905.

Bottom: The buses were also used for tourism, as here on the Three Rivers Tour. Despite wanting to extend further down the Dee, the railway was not allowed but the bus service was welcomed by locals and tourists alike.

Enjoying the "Three Rivers Tour." Castle Newe in the Distance.

Great North of Scotland

DEESIDE

Aberdeen to Banchory

Leaving GUILD station at Aberdeen, we proceed to RUTHRIESTON, thence to CULTS, so named from 'Quiques,' a corner, which has a fine church, the living of which was held by WIlkie's father, who with his son were natives. Close at hand is Walter Hill, with a Roman camp, and Cranford Priory, the seat of Lady M. Cranford – and quickly reach MURTLE; from thence the train proceeds to MILLTIMBER, and then arrives at

CULTER

Telegraph station at Aberdeen, 7¾ miles.

Here are paper and saw mills, and close at hand is Culter House, the seat of J. Duff, Esq.

Passing DRUM, close to which is Drumoak, the seat of A. Irvine, Esq., which has an old tower with walls 12 feet thick, we arrive at PARK station, and thence forward to MILLS of DRUM; leaving which, we soon reach

BANCHORY TERNAN

A telegraph station. HOTEL – Douglas' Arms.

Banchory Ternan, or Upper Banchory, is a small village on the banks of the Dee, at the confluence of that river with the Feugh. In the vicinity are Banchory Cottage and Inchmarlo, the seat of D. Davidson, Esq.

GLASSELS and TORPHINS stations.

LUMPHANAN – Here is shown Macbeth's cairn, a heap 120 feet high.

DESS station.

ABOYNE

The terminus of the railway, and beautifully situated at the confluence of the Tanar with the Dee, and surrounded with hills thickly covered with wood on every side. Aboyne Castle, a seat of the Marquis of Huntly, is close at hand. It offers an excellent starting point for the tourist to visit the picturesque scenery extending between Ballater, Braemar, and Balmoral.

Above: An advantage of being King is that you can have whatever you want. Here is King Edward VII's Foden steam lorry at Balmoral.

Left: Bucksburn has been famed for its paper mills for centuries. It was a dangerous trade and men would often lose an arm in the rollers, as shown here.

Port Henry Harbour. Peterhead

Lower left: Peterhead is still renowed for its fishing industry, and is one of Britian's most important deep-sea ports.

BALLATER

This watering place, which is close to the Pannanich Springs, is the Tunbridge Wells and Keswick of Aberdeenshire, where people go to drink the waters and enjoy the walks and excursions among the neighbouring hills, from some of which (Craigendarroch in particular) there are extensive and beautiful views. The objects of interest in the district are – the Bum of the Vat, a natural wall of perpendicular rock; Lochnagar, which commands a splendid prospect; the Linn and Loch of Muich, and the Dhu Loch; and lastly, Mount Keen.

Ballater to Balmoral and Braemar

Following the course of the Dee, the coach proceeds along the south bank)past Abergeldie Castle), formerly the seat of M. F. Gordon, Esq., which has an old tower among the birches, and belonged to H.R.H. the late Duchess of Kent, to Crathie, the castle of which (an old Flemish house), is the seat of Sir R. Burnett, Bart., a small village on the north side of the river, in the vicinity of which are Invercauld, J. Farquharson, Esq., Malcolm Canmore's hunting seat, Monaltrie, Marr Lodge, Duke of Leeds, and the salmon fisheries. About a quarter of a mile beyond is the summer residence of Her Majesty, Balmoral Castle, situated in a picturesque vale or dell, surrounded by beautiful mountain scenery; and close by is Birkhill, which belonged to the late Prince Consort.

CASTLETON OF BRAEMAR

HOTELS – Invereauld Arms, Fife Arms.

This is only an old Highland village, surrounded by mountains, and situated in the centre of a region of forests; but it is the best place for the tourist to select and to start from on a visit to the different excursions and places of interest in the neighbourhood. Braemar Castle, and view from Invercauld Bridge; the Falls of the Garrawalt, and Corriemulzie, the Linns of Quoich and Dee, are the nearest excursions. The more distant are Lochnagar, and other peaks in Glen Tilt, and beyond Ben Macdhui, in the heart of the magnificent scenery of the Grampians. The latter, to the south of Braemar, is 4,390 feet high, or second only to Ben Nevis, the highest mountain of Great Britain.

Great North of Scotland

Aberdeen to Keith

Passing the intermediate stations of KITTYBREWSTER, WOODSIDE, and BUXBURN, we arrive at the station of

DYCE, where are a Druid circle of 10 stones, on Tirebeggar Hill; Dyce House, seat of Gordon Skene, Esq.; and a fine church with an old font. It is also the junction of the Buchan section of this railway. The line runs a distance of 38 miles to ...

PETERHEAD, a town of some importance, situated on a rich and fertile plain. It has its mineral springs, sea bathing, fisheries, and other appliances of a commercial character. Again on the main line, we pass the station of KINALDIE, and arrive at

KINTORE
Telegraph station at Inverury, 3 miles.

This was formerly a forest, and had a hunting seat given by Bruce to the Keiths. In the vicinity are Thainston, seat of D. Mitchell, Esq., Castle-hill Law, Bruce's Howe, some Cairns and the remains of four Druid circles.

Alford Valley
This is a railway 16½ miles long, having on its route the stations of KEMNAY, MONYMUSK, TILLIFOWRIE, and WHITEHOUSE, and terminating at

ALFORD
A place remarkable for the defeat of the Covenanters by Montrose in 1645. It is situated on the Don, in which are salmon fisheries, and has a fair once a month for cattle.

Great North of Scotland continued

INVERURY
POPULATION, about 2,649. A telegraph station.
HOTEL – Kintore Arms. MARKET DAY – Saturday.
FAIRS – Every month or fortnight.

Here Bruce defeated the Comyn. In the vicinity are Keith Hall, Earl of Kintore.
From this point a branch turns off to the right, through LETHENTY to OLD MELDRUM, a distance 5¾ miles.
INVERAMSAY station.

BANFF, MACDUFF, and TURRIFF JUNCTION
WARTLE, ROTHIE, and FYVIE stations.
AUCHTERLESS, on the river Ythan, in which pearls have been known to be found, and in which there are salmon fisheries.

TURRIFF
Telegraph station at Banff, 11½ miles.

Population about 1,650, engaged in the manufacture of thread and linen. Situated on the river Deveron, in which are salmon and trout.

PLAIDY and KING EDWARD station.

BANFF

A telegraph station. MARKET DAY – Friday.

FAIRS – January 7th; February 1st, Tuesday, o.s.; May, Tuesday, on or after the 26th; August 1st, Friday, o.s.; November, Friday before the 22nd.

A parliamentary borough and Coast Guard station, at the mouth of the river Deveron. It has a population of about 6,000 engaged in the fisheries, and to a limited extent in the manufacture of leather, linen, &c. The extensive park and mansion of the Earl of Fife is in the vicinity. Its situation commands a series of beautiful views, and it possesses a good gallery of pictures.

Great North of Scotland Main Line continued

Passing PITCAPLE, the seat of M. Lumsden, Esq., we proceed to OYNE, near which are Pittodrie, sent of R. Erskine, Esq. and Tillyfour, R. Grant, Esq., and reach BUCHANSTONE; thence to

INSCH, close to which is Craigievar, the seat of Sir W. Forbes, Bart.; here fairs are held, on Friday before 18th May and November, 3rd Wednesday in May, and 3rd Tuesday in October, after which the train arrives at WARDHOUSE, and then proceeds on to the

KENNETHMONT and GARTLEY stations, near which are excellent trout streams, and the fine old ruin Gartley Place, the ancient seat of the Gordons, now belonging to the Duke of Richmond. Soon afterwards we stop at

HUNTLY

POPULATION about 4,061. A telegraph station.

HOTEL – Gordon Arms, W. Beattie. MARKET DAY – Thursday.

FAIRS – Last Wed. in Jan., last Tues. in Feb. and March, Wed. before May 26th, last Tues. in May, 2nd Tues. in June, 3rd Tues., in June, Wed. after 1st Tues. in July, Wed. after 2nd Tues. in Aug and Sept., 4th Tues. in Sept., Thurs. Before Nov. 22nd, 1st Tues. in Nov. And Dec.

Huntly is a picturesque village, standing on a point of land formed by the confluence of the Bogie with the Deveron, where there is an excellent garnet, trout, and salmon fishing. It contains the ruins of Huntly Castle, the two halls and gate of which still remain. Huntly Lodge, the Duke of Richmond's seat, is close at hand, and also the splendid modern mansion of the present Marquis of Huntly.

From hence the line continues through ROTHIEMAY to GRANGE, the point of junction with the

BANFF, PORTSOY, and STRATHISLA

This is a line 16¼ miles long, passing through KNOCK and CORNHILL to TILLYNAUGHT, where the line turns to the left, a distance of 2¾ miles, to the harbour at PORTSOY, a seaport of growing importance. The continuation of the line from Tillynaught is via LADY'S BRIDGE to the harbour at

BANFF, see above.

Great North of Scotland Main Line continued

KEITH

A telegraph station.

A small town of about 1,800 inhabitants, consisting only of one long street. The church stands of the site of a very old one, and was rebuilt, in a pointed style, in 1819. The tower is 104 feet high. Ferguson, the astronomer, was born here.

KEITH AND DUFFTOWN

This is a line of about nine miles, and passes through EARLSMILL, AUCHINDACHY, and DRUMMUIR, to the little village of

DUFFTOWN, situated on the river Spey, at the foot of a range of hills, the principal and centre of which is Benrinnes, which rises to the height of about 2,700 feet. A little further south lies Glenlivet, the scene of Argyll's defeat, when he fought against the Catholic leaders.

A short line to the right unites this place with the Morayshire railway at Strathspey.

MORAYSHIRE

Is now divided into three several shires, viz., Banff, Moray, and Nairn. In describing this beautiful district of country, known by the name of Morayshire, it is usual to include the small county of Nairn with which it is intimately connected. Some parts of this district partake of the wild, rocky, and mountainous character of the Highlands. The low country is a large plain extending from the Spey westward, between the shore and a range of mountains for nearly forty miles. This plain, however, is diversified over its whole extent by short ridges of lower hills, in general nearly parallel to the shore. There are many plains in the course of the Spey, and some of the tract of the Findhorn, of great fertility and beauty. It returns one member in conjunction with Nairn.